Play Safe – and Win

Many years ago someone pinned a message on the notice-board of a London club: 'Spades breaking badly today'. It was intended as a joke, of course, but it was observed that members handled their spades with particular care for the rest of the day.

Anyone can make contracts when all the finesses are right and the suits break kindly. It is what happens when conditions are less favourable that separates the men from the boys. The expert is a confirmed pessimist who expects finesses to fail and all suits (not just spades) to break badly. By taking timely precautions he is often able to nullify, or at least mitigate, the effects of the bad breaks.

The right precautions to take are fully explained in this book. With the help of more than a hundred examples, the authors show how bad breaks may be overcome and losing finesses avoided.

Eric Jannersten, many times Swedish Champion, is a bridge journalist of world renown and a teacher who has set more than 250,000 pupils on the road to good bridge. He has written a number of books in collaboration with Jan Wohlin, who is a European Champion and a first-class analyst.

By the same authors

WINNING PAIRS TECHNIQUE

Play Safe – and Win

ERIC JANNERSTEN
and
JAN WOHLIN

Translated by Hugh Kelsey

LONDON
VICTOR GOLLANCZ LTD
in association with Peter Crawley
1981

ISBN 0 575 03006 2

Filmset by Willmer Brothers Limited,
Birkenhead, Merseyside
Printed in Great Britain by
St Edmundsbury Press Limited,
Bury St Edmunds, Suffolk

Contents

Foreword

Safety play at bridge is a concept that covers a great deal of ground. It encompasses the handling of a single suit, where the plan must be to make the contract no matter how the opposing cards are distributed, and it also extends to the overall play of the hand, where due regard has to be paid to the probabilities in determining the safest line.

One thing is clear. Safety play has nothing whatever to do with making as many tricks as possible. I wrote somewhere that as dummy lays down his cards on the table he should simultaneously display a notice-board bearing the following legend in letters of fire: "Play for the contract and damn the overtricks!" This exhortation does not apply in pairs tournaments, of course. Pairs scoring compels one to abandon safety, but in "real" bridge the letters of fire should be heeded. There is so little to gain and so much to lose in trying for overtricks. The skilful player displays what might be thought to be an exaggerated pessimism in the play of the cards. His path is bordered by trolls and goblins. He sees ghosts in full daylight and imagines dangers lurking around every corner. All suits will break badly and not a finesse will succeed: that is the expert's starting point. As the play proceeds he has to modify this negative attitude if he is not to concede defeat in advance, but at the back of his mind he is constantly planning how to overcome the malice of the Goddess of cards.

Often—far too often in the view of the master—the average player achieves the same result as the careful expert by playing in poppa-momma fashion. On those occasions when accuracy pays off, the average player complains about his notorious bad luck while the expert explains that technique has at last reaped its reward.

Although careful play may not be decisive in terms of points, it is always worth while. There is a great pleasure in finding the one line of play that makes a certainty of the contract against any defence and distribution. The satisfaction of having done one's best, even if success does not crown one's efforts, is a reward in itself.

This book is a collaboration. I am responsible for the text and Jan Wohlin for the illustrating examples, in which the reader always occupies the South seat at rubber or team bridge. Enjoy yourself!

Eric Jannersten

Suit Management

In theory one should stick to the mathematical probabilities at the bridge table when it is a matter of securing a certain number of tricks from a suit. In practical bridge, however, a number of other factors come into play. Inferences can be drawn from the bidding, and the division of the opponents' cards can often be worked out from what has happened in the play so far. One talks therefore of probabilities *a priori*, that is to say when no external influences upset the conditions. When something happens during the course of the play, these original probabilities change.

Not only in the matter of handling a single suit but also when one is planning the complete play of the hand from the first trick, it is useful to know just how likely it is that a suit will be divided in one way or another. The rule of thumb says that when the defenders have an odd number of cards in a suit they are likely to be divided as evenly as possible, while an even number of cards are likely to split unevenly, with one defender having more cards in the suit than the other. With the values rounded up or down to even numbers, the probable divisions of a particular number of cards in two hands are as follows:

Seven cards missing:

4–3	62%
5–2	31%
6–1	7%
7–0	0% (for practical purposes)

The probability of the opponents' seven cards dividing in the most even possible way is therefore 62% for and 38% against.

Six cards missing:

4–2	48%
3–3	36%
5–1	15%
6–0	1%

That the opponents' six cards will divide evenly, three in each hand, is only a 36% chance. There is a probability of 64% that they will divide in some other way.

Five cards missing:

3–2	68%
4–1	28%
5–0	4%

One often has an eight-card trump suit and the risk of running into a bad break is quite considerable. The friendly 3–2 break is normal, but in one deal in three the suit will break badly.

Four cards missing:

3–1	50%
2–2	40%
4–0	10%

You might think that the opponents would normally have two cards each, but the odds are 3 to 2 against this.

Three cards missing:

2–1	78%
3–0	22%

You must reckon on finding one of the opponents with a void in rather more than one deal in five.

Two cards missing:
1–1	52%
2–0	48%

Here it is pretty much a toss-up whether the cards will be distributed in one way or the other. The scales tip slightly in favour of the even split. If the king is missing, there is a shade of odds in favour of playing for the drop rather than finessing. In the following position one plays for the hearts to be 1–1.

$\heartsuit$ Q 10 7 4 3

$\heartsuit$ A J 9 8 6 2

Here and in the examples that follow we assume that there are plenty of entries to both hands in the outside suits.

There is one small reservation about playing for the drop in hearts. The right play is to enter dummy in another suit and play the queen. It is conceivable that East, holding both king and five, will make the mistake of covering the queen. The additional chance cost nothing. If East plays the five, of course, you go up with the ace.

In that example you had everything to gain and nothing to lose by trying for the maximum. Often, however, there will be a decision to make about how a suit should be handled, and the right method will depend on the number of tricks you need from the suit.

$\heartsuit$ Q 9 6 4 3

$\heartsuit$ A J 8 5 2

You cannot afford to lose a trick. Start with the queen from dummy and run it if East plays low. You will bring in the suit without loss as long as the king is with East. If he covers the queen, your ace wins and you are in a position to take a further finesse against the ten if West shows out.

$$\heartsuit \; Q\,9\,6\,4\,3$$

$$\heartsuit \; A\,10\,8\,5\,2$$

Needing five tricks, you should start with the ace. It could be right to start with the queen from dummy, running it if East played low. You would then succeed if West had the singleton jack. However, there is twice as good a chance of finding someone with a single king as there is of finding just West with a single jack.

If the situation is such that you can afford to lose one heart trick but on no account two, you can solve the problem by playing a low heart from the table and just covering the card East plays. East is thus restricted to one heart trick when he has all three missing cards. If East shows out on the first round, you play the ace and continue the suit. West can make no more than his king.

$$\diamondsuit \; K\,J\,8\,5\,2$$

$$\diamondsuit \; 10\,7\,6\,4\,3$$

In this example you can afford to lose only one diamond trick. Play a low card from hand and finesse the jack if West plays the nine. Singleton ace and singleton queen with East are both equally likely. What gives the finesse of the jack an advantage is that West may have A Q 9. When East shows out on the first round, you can return to hand in a side suit and play another diamond towards dummy.

$$\diamondsuit \; A\,Q\,10\,6\,4$$

$$\diamondsuit \; 7\,5\,3\,2$$

If you need five diamond tricks, play towards dummy and finesse the queen. You will succeed when West has the king doubleton or East the jack singleton. If you can afford to lose one diamond trick but no more, start with the ace to guard against a singleton king in the East hand. If no honour appears, return to your own hand and play another diamond towards dummy's queen.

♣ A 9 3 2

♣ K Q 10 5 4

In this diagram you can guarantee five club tricks by starting with one of the top honours from your own hand. Then it is just a momentary annoyance if someone shows out. Whoever has the club length, you can finesse against the jack and avoid the loss of a trick.

♠ A 9 3 2

♠ K Q 8 5 4

This situation is so similar to the last that it is often misplayed. There is a risk of losing a spade trick only if the suit breaks 4–0. If West has the length there is nothing to be done. Spade length with East can be dealt with, however, provided that you start with dummy's ace. With both spade honours in your hand intact, East's jack and ten can be picked up by finessing.

◇ A K 7 4 2

◇ 10 8 5 3

Needing all the tricks, you must cash the ace and king in the hope that the suit breaks 2–2. If you can afford to lose one trick in the suit but not two, you should start with a low diamond from hand, inserting the seven from dummy if West plays the six. This protects against all four diamonds in the West hand.

◇ Q 8 4

◇ A 10 7 5 3 2

When you cannot afford to lose a diamond trick you must start with the queen from dummy in the hope of finding West with a singleton jack. If East covers with the king and the jack falls under the ace, you return to dummy to take a further finesse against East's nine.

There is no profit in starting with the ace of diamonds. Even if a singleton king falls from some quarter, the other defender will have a sure stopper left with his J 9.

♡ A K 4

♡ 9 8 7 6 5 2

If you need to make six heart tricks the suit will have to divide 2–2. If five heart tricks are all you need, you should lead the two of hearts from hand and finesse dummy's four if West plays the three. You thereby protect against West having all four missing hearts.

Should West play a higher heart on your two and East show out when you win on the table, you can return to hand and lead another heart to hold West to one trick in the suit.

♠ 10 4

♠ A Q 7 6 5 3 2

Needing to avoid the loss of a spade trick, you must hope that the suit is divided 2–2 with the king in the East hand. Play a spade from dummy for a finesse of the queen.

The safest way of avoiding the loss of more than one spade

trick is to start with the ace. This guards against the possibility of a singleton king with West. If no honour appears on the first round, cross to dummy and lead a second spade towards your queen.

If you are in the fortunate position of being able to afford two spade losers but not three, you should start with a small spade from hand. No matter if someone shows out, you will have no problems with the continuation. This careful play guards against all four spades in the West hand. West would make three tricks if you tackled the suit in any other way.

$$\diamond \text{ K 8 3 2}$$

$$\diamond \text{ A 10 7 6 4}$$

Irrespective of the number of tricks required, it is right to start with a low card from hand. If West shows out, you win with the king and hold East to one trick in the suit by leading twice through his honours.

If West plays an honour on the first round, the king wins and you continue with a finesse of the ten. In this you are following the principle of free choice. With queen–jack doubleton and a free choice of card to play, West would presumably play the queen half the time and the jack half the time. With a singleton honour he has no choice but to play it, and the latter holding is the more probable.

$$\clubsuit \text{ J 8 5 2}$$

$$\clubsuit \text{ A Q 7 4 3}$$

Needing five club tricks, you can either play a low card from the table for a finesse of the queen, or lead the jack with the intention of running it if East fails to cover. In the latter case you are playing for West to have the singleton nine or ten. When East covers the jack and the nine or ten falls under the ace, you plan to return to dummy for a further finesse against East.

The two lines of play are roughly equal in merit as one can see by setting out all the possible distributions.

—	K 10 9 6
6	K 10 9
9	K 10 6
10	K 9 6
K	10 9 6
9 6	K 10
10 6	K 9
K 6	10 9
10 9	K 6
K 9	10 6
K 10	9 6
10 9 6	K
K 9 6	10
K 10 6	9
K 10 9	6
K 10 9 6	—

The four cards can be distributed in these sixteen ways. Starting with the jack is the only winning move in two of the cases—where West has the singleton nine or ten. It loses a trick in two other cases, however—where East has the singleton king or the doubleton K 6—when the play of a low card for a finesse of the queen is the right move. Since the doubleton holdings have a slightly higher frequency (one sixth of 40%) than the singletons (one eighth of 50%), it might appear that the play of a low card for a finesse of the queen has a slight edge.

Not so. It is right to lead the jack from the table, for you thereby hold your losers in the suit to one trick if you are unlucky enough to find West with a void. A direct finesse of the queen then gives East two tricks. If you can afford to lose one trick in the suit, therefore, it is vital to start with dummy's jack.

$$\diamondsuit \text{ K J 4 2}$$

$$\diamondsuit \text{ A 9 6 5 3}$$

Needing five diamond tricks, you should play for the drop in the absence of any indications to the contrary. But if you need to make sure of just four diamond tricks, you should start with dummy's king. Should East happen to have all the outstanding diamonds, you can hold him to one trick by leading next towards your ace–nine. If it is West who has all the diamonds, you take the ace on the second round and then play towards dummy's jack. West can have one trick with his queen but no more.

$$\spadesuit \text{ K J 7 6 2}$$

$$\spadesuit \text{ Q 8 5 3}$$

In this combination you should start with the queen of spades. On learning that East is void, you can see to it that West's ten and nine are finessed out. If it is West who is void there is no way of avoiding the loss of two tricks in the suit.

$$\clubsuit \text{ A J 5 2}$$

$$\clubsuit \text{ Q 6 4 3}$$

If you need four club tricks, the only chance is that West has the doubleton king. Start with a finesse of the jack and hope for the king to fall on the second round.

The right play when you can afford to lose one club trick is to start with the ace. This guards against a singleton king in the East hand.

$$\diamondsuit \text{ A J 4 3}$$

$$\diamondsuit \text{ Q 10 5 2}$$

Start with a small card from hand and finesse dummy's jack. If this goes well, return to hand and lead the queen or ten for another finesse. You have protected against a singleton king with West, in which case starting with an honour card promotes a trick for East.

$$\heartsuit \text{ A Q 10 4 2}$$

$$\heartsuit \text{ 6 5 3}$$

You can make five heart tricks only if the cards are divided 3–2 with both king and jack in the West hand. Start with a finesse of dummy's ten. If it wins, return to hand and play another heart for a finesse of the queen.

The method of play is different if four heart tricks are all you need. Now you finesse the queen of hearts on the first round. This protects against the following layout:

$$\heartsuit \text{ A Q 10 4 2}$$

$$\heartsuit \text{ K 9 8 7} \qquad \heartsuit \text{ J}$$

$$\heartsuit \text{ 6 5 3}$$

If you finesse the ten you must lose two heart tricks. It is true that East might have the singleton king, but in that case you must lose two heart tricks whether you finesse the queen or the ten.

It looks as though you should be able to guard against either king or jack singleton in the East hand by starting with the ace. If nothing significant happens, you can return to hand and play another heart for a finesse of the ten, protecting against four cards with both honours in the West hand. However, a 3–2 break is much commoner than 4–1, as you know. When you finesse the ten East may make an unnecessary trick with his doubleton jack. You might, of course, have played the queen from dummy, but with your famous luck East would then have turned up with a doubleton king. You guard against unlucky guesses of this sort by playing for split honours from the beginning and starting with a finesse of the queen.

$$\diamond \text{ K 9 5}$$

$$\diamond \text{ A J 4 3 2}$$

In no trumps, needing five diamond tricks, you start with a low card to the king and finesse the jack on the next round. You achieve the desired result in one half of the 3–2 breaks— 34% or roughly one time in three.

If you can afford to lose one trick but not two, you start with the ace and continue with a low card towards dummy. If West plays low you finesse the nine. If West proves to have a singleton diamond, you win the second round with the king and return a diamond towards your jack. This method of play guarantees four diamond tricks against all possible 4–1 breaks.

$$\clubsuit \text{ 9 5 4}$$

$$\clubsuit \text{ A K 10 3 2}$$

Needing all five club tricks, you should play low from the table and finesse the ten. You will succeed when the suit divides 3–2 and East has both honours.

If you can afford the loss of one club trick, you should start with the ace. When no honour appears, continue with a low

card towards the nine. This ensures four tricks whenever East
has four clubs and also when he has a singleton honour.

♠ A 10 6 3

♠ J 5 4 2

If you need three spade tricks the best chance is to play low
from hand for a finesse of dummy's ten. Assuming East wins
the trick, play the ace when you regain the lead. You will
succeed in those 3–2 breaks where West has a doubleton
honour, both honours, and three small, giving you a better
than one in three chance of success.

If you need only to make sure of two tricks, there is no
problem when the suit breaks 3–2. The 4–1 divisions need not
trouble you either. Just start with the ace of spades and
continue with a low card towards your jack. You have
protected yourself against a singleton honour in either hand
and you cannot be denied two tricks.

♠ J 6

♠ A Q 7 4 3 2

The defenders are bound to make at least one trick in this
suit however you play. The right move is to start with the ace,
guarding against a singleton king in either hand. If nothing
happens you must hope for the suit to divide 3–2.

Strengthen the South hand fractionally by substituting the
five of spades for the four and a different method of play is
required.

♠ J 6

♠ A Q 7 5 3 2

Now you should start with the jack from dummy, guarding against the possibility of West having the singleton eight, nine or ten. The picture may be like this:

♠ J 6

♠ 9   ♠ K 10 8 4

♠ A Q 7 5 3 2

The jack is covered by the king and ace, and when West drops one of the intermediate cards you cross back to dummy and play the six of spades for a finesse against East.

Your play will fail if either defender has the singleton king, but it is more probable in the ratio of 3 to 2 that West will have a middle singleton.

♡ A 7

♡ K 10 8 6 4 2

If you need six heart tricks there is nothing for it but to play off the ace and king, hoping for the queen and jack to fall. To protect against the loss of two heart tricks, the right play is to start with the ten from your own hand. If West plays the queen, jack or nine, you go up with the ace and run the seven of hearts on the way back if East does not cover.

If West plays a low heart on your ten, you play the seven from dummy. This guards against a singleton nine in the East hand.

◇ 9 7 4 3 2

◇ A K 6

Suppose you need four diamond tricks. No problem if the suit divides 3–2. If it is 4–1, the only chance is to find West with the singleton eight. So you start with the nine from the table, running it if East plays low. More likely East will cover the nine, forcing you to win with the king. Now, if the eight drops from West, you return to dummy and play another diamond, compelling East to split his equals and holding him to one trick in the suit.

♠ A 10 5 2

♠ K J 7 3

You need four spade tricks and, missing five cards including the queen, it is right to finesse. In which direction do you take the finesse?

No, it is not an occasion for tossing a coin. If the spades are 3–2 all you need it to guess right, but someone may have four cards including the queen. In that case you can make four tricks only if West has the singleton eight or nine.

♠ A 10 5 2

♠ 8   ♠ Q 9 6 4

♠ K J 7 3

The right way of handling the suit is to play the ace and continue with the ten, running it if East plays low. If East covers with the queen your king wins, and when West shows out you can return to dummy to finesse against East's nine (or eight, as the case may be).

♣ A 8 5 2

♣ K J 6 3

If you need four club tricks there is nothing for it but to hope for a 3–2 split and the queen with East. You start with the ace and continue with a finesse of the jack. The safest way of trying for three tricks, however, is to start with the king, which protects against a singleton ten or nine with East. The situation may be:

♣ A 8 5 2

♣ Q 9 7 4   ♣ 10

♣ K J 6 3

When the ten (or the nine) drops under the king of clubs, three tricks in the suit are guaranteed. You continue with a low card, and when West follows you cover his card as cheaply as possible.

If both defenders follow low on the first round, you continue with a club to the ace. You are sure of three tricks as long as East is not now void.

◇ K Q 5 4

◇ 7 6 3 2

If you need three diamond tricks you have to rely on a 3–2 break and the ace with West. Play towards one of dummy's honours and, if it wins the trick, repeat the manoeuvre.

If you need only two diamond tricks it is right to start with a low card from both hands. You thereby guard against the following distribution:

◇ K Q 5 4

◇ J 10 9 8   ◇ A

◇ 7 6 3 2

If the defenders are able to win the trick cheaply, you next play a diamond towards dummy, and you can repeat this manoeuvre if West turns up with four diamonds.

♠ K J 5 4

♠ 7 6 3 2

Needing three spade tricks, you must hope that West has two or three spades including the ace and queen. Start with a low card for a finesse of the jack, and next time lead towards the king.

If two spade tricks are enough for the contract, you should start with a low card towards dummy's king. This guards against a singleton queen with East. If the king wins and East follows with a low card, you next play towards dummy's jack, protecting against a small singleton in the East hand.

♡ A J 5 4

♡ 7 6 3 2

The chance of making three heart tricks is not great. Play a low card from hand and finesse dummy's jack. East could have king–queen doubleton, to be sure, but it is three times as probable that West will have both honours plus a small card.

If two heart tricks are enough, start with the ace to guard against a singleton honour with East. If no honour drops, return to hand and play another heart towards the jack. You will still make two tricks if the suit breaks 3–2 or if West has the length.

♡ A J 3

♡ 10 6 5 4 2

The best chance of making four heart tricks is to play low towards dummy for a finesse of the jack. On the next round you play the ace, and you will succeed when West has a doubleton honour, when he has both honours and not more than three cards in the suit, and when East has both honours doubleton.

If two heart tricks will do, it is safest to start with the ace, protecting against a singleton honour with East. If no honour drops, you return to hand and play another heart towards the jack, ensuring that West can make no more than two heart tricks if he started with four cards including the king and queen.

♣ K 10 5 3 2

♣ J 6 4

The cards will need to lie well if you require four club tricks. Play a low card from hand for a finesse of the ten. If this draws the ace, play the king on the next round hoping to fell the doubleton queen in the West hand. If the ten of clubs wins, return to hand and play another club towards the king. You will succeed if West started with ace, queen and another.

If you need only three club tricks, the safest play is to put up the king on the first round. This protects against the loss of a trick to the singleton queen in the East hand.

◇ A Q 6 4 2

◇ 7 5 3

Needing four diamond tricks you must hope for a 3–2 break. If the king is with East, you have a chance only when it is doubleton. The right move is to start with a low diamond from the table. Your intention is to finesse the queen on the second round. However, the distribution may be as follows:

◇ A Q 6 4 2

◇ J 9 8   ◇ K 10

◇ 7 5 3

What will East do when you play a low diamond from the table? In practical play he will almost invariably take his king for fear of losing it altogether if you are leading towards the jack.

The same principle applies in the next example:

♠ K 10 9 8

♠ A 3 2

From a purely mathematical point of view the best chance of making three spade tricks lies in starting with the ace and then finessing twice against West. It is only if East has the queen and jack guarded that you will be defeated. As before, however, you gain extra psychological chances by starting from the table. The layout may be as follows:

♠ K 10 9 8

♠ 7 5 4   ♠ Q J 6

♠ A 3 2

You play the ten of spades from the table intending to go up with the ace. As long as you don't think out loud, East remains unaware of your intention. He will not take the risk of losing his spade trick completely by playing low. He will cover the ten of spades, thus solving the problem for you. If East is good enough to play the six of spades without hesitation, he deserves to be rewarded by making a trick more than he really should make.

♣ A 5 3

♣ K J 4 2

Four club tricks can be made only if the suit breaks 3–3 and the queen is with East. After the ace of clubs you take a second-round finesse of the jack, hoping for the queen to fall under your king. The chance of success is 18%.

To give yourself the greatest chance of making three tricks you should start with the king and then play low to the ace, guarding against the possibility of a doubleton queen in the West hand. If no queen appears on the first two rounds, you continue with a club from the table towards your jack. You will fail to make three tricks only when West started with four or more clubs including the queen.

These are just a few of the many suit combinations in which safety play can be applied to give the best chance of making the required number of tricks. Once the principles are understood, it is not too hard to work out the appropriate safety play for each individual case. With experience comes the ability to choose the right method almost automatically.

Guarding Against a Ruff

Often there is reason to suspect that the defenders are angling for a ruff. Usually one hastens to draw trumps, but occasionally one has to look around for other counter-measures.

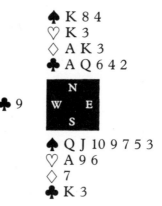

♠ K 8 4
♥ K 3
♦ A K 3
♣ A Q 6 4 2

♣ 9

♠ Q J 10 9 7 5 3
♥ A 9 6
♦ 7
♣ K 3

South plays in six spades and West leads the nine of clubs. Only the ace of trumps is missing, and South, lulled into a sense of false security, may be tempted to lead a trump at trick two. If he does he will be swiftly disillusioned. The contract is defeated when the complete deal turns out to be:

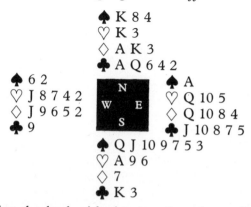

East gains the lead with the ace of spades and gives his partner a club ruff.

It is this sort of unpleasant surprise that the experienced player tries to guard against. The more secure a contract appears to be, the more he worries that some misery may be lurking in the bushes. South curses his ineptitude in not bidding the slam in no trumps where no ruff could threaten the twelfth trick. When his annoyance has cooled, he weighs the chances and reaches the conclusion that it is infinitely more likely that the clubs are 5–1 than that the diamonds are 8–1. Before touching trumps, therefore, he plays off the ace and king of diamonds, discarding his second club. Now he can safely let the opponents in with the ace of trumps, for he can ruff the club return high and make the rest of the tricks with ease.

Love all.
Dealer South.

S	W	N	E
1 ♡	pass	2 ◇	2 ♠
4 ♡	pass	5 ♣	pass
6 ♡	pass	pass	pass

West leads the three of spades. How do you plan the play?

For a start, don't make the mistake of automatically playing a card from the table. Make it a habit always to form a plan of play as soon as dummy appears. A bad plan is better than no plan at all. The time spent on early planning always comes back, usually with interest, in the later stages of the play.

What does an experienced player make of the opening lead of the three of spades. Well, he acknowledges that it has "singleton" written all over it. East made an overcall in spades, after all, and the spade two is visible in dummy. No further evidence is needed. The slam appears to be doomed, and nothing short of a drastic rescue manoeuvre is likely to alter your fate. The only chance lies in trying to create some confusion for East.

Having made up your mind, you play a low card from the table. On East's ace of spades you drop the king without batting an eye. Now look at the situation from East's point of view. The complete deal is:

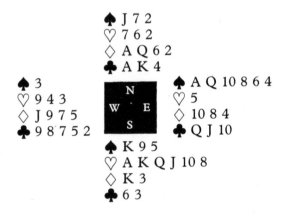

It appears to East that his partner has led low from 9 5 3 in order to show his length. East does not dare continue the suit for fear that dummy's jack of spades will give you an extra trick. Probably he will switch to the queen of clubs, and now the slam has at least a short reprieve.

There are only eleven tricks, and the best way of trying for a twelfth lies in a double squeeze. You test the trumps with the ace and king, learning as expected that East is short in hearts. It seems unlikely that East will have diamond length, so you prepare for the double squeeze by playing off the three top diamonds, discarding a spade from your hand. You return to hand with the third round of hearts and play off the rest of your trumps.

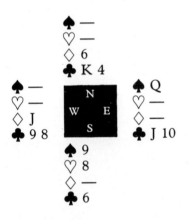

When you play your last trump in the above position, West has to throw a club in order to keep his diamond guard. You discard the diamond from dummy and East is sunk.

Perhaps it is wrong to call this a safety play. But the surest way of going down in the slam is to hang on to the king of spades at trick one. Once the initial deception succeeds, the line of play that gives the best chance is the double squeeze. The diamond length is more likely to be with West than with East, who is known to have six spades. If East had held four diamonds, a simple squeeze in spades and diamonds would have been the winning line.

On that hand you could not afford to draw trumps at once in spite of the threat of a ruff. In the next case you have to leave the trumps alone for another reason.

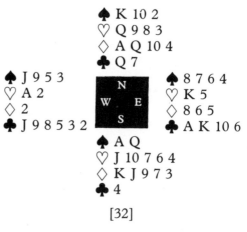

♠ K 10 2
♡ Q 9 8 3
◇ A Q 10 4
♣ Q 7

◇ 2

♠ A Q
♡ J 10 7 6 4
◇ K J 9 7 3
♣ 4

Game all.
Dealer South.

S	W	N	E
1 ♡	pass	3 ♡	pass
4 ♡	pass	pass	pass

West leads the two of diamonds. Plan the play.

The defenders have two quick tricks in trumps and one in clubs. That two of diamonds smells of a singleton, and a ruff may defeat the contract. East must have at least one of the top clubs, and if you start on trumps you are likely to go down. What you must do is try to destroy the enemy communications in clubs. The ruff will probably be averted if the defenders can communicate only in trumps.

Your chance lies in finding trumps 2–2 with divided honours, or three trumps including both honours with West. Also West will need to have the spade jack. The complete deal could be:

♠ K 10 2
♡ Q 9 8 3
◇ A Q 10 4
♣ Q 7

♠ J 9 5 3   ♠ 8 7 6 4
♡ A 2   ♡ K 5
◇ 2   ◇ 8 6 5
♣ J 9 8 5 3 2 ♣ A K 10 6

♠ A Q
♡ J 10 7 6 4
◇ K J 9 7 3
♣ 4

To begin with you play the queen of diamonds from the table in an attempt to camouflage the situation from East, who may receive the impression that his partner has led away from the king. After a spade to the ace, you overtake the queen of spades with dummy's king in order to continue with the ten of spades. When East plays low on the third round you are half-way home. You discard the losing club from hand and West wins his jack of spades. You ruff the club return, and at last it is time to tackle the trumps. West has no opportunity to ruff a diamond except with his master ace of trumps, and the game is made.

```
            ♠ 10 9 6 3 2
            ♡ A J 7 5
            ◇ A Q
            ♣ 6 3
                   N
      ♣ K    W         E
                   S
            ♠ A K Q 4
            ♡ K 8 2
Game all.   ◇ K J 5
Dealer South. ♣ J 9 2
```

S	W	N	E
1 NT	pass	2 ♣	pass
2 ♠	pass	4 ♠	pass
pass	pass		

This example comes from an English International Trial of some years ago. East overtook his partner's lead of the king of clubs with the ace and returned the seven of clubs. West captured the nine with his ten and continued with the club queen. South tried the ten of spades from the table, but East over-ruffed with the jack and exited with a trump. After drawing trumps South was forced to fall back upon the heart finesse, and East took the setting trick with the queen of hearts.

The complete deal was as follows:

[33]

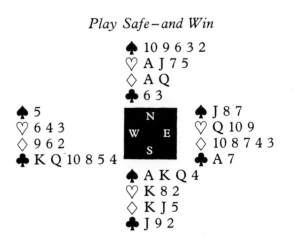

♠ 10 9 6 3 2
♡ A J 7 5
◇ A Q
♣ 6 3

♠ 5   ♠ J 8 7
♡ 6 4 3   ♡ Q 10 9
◇ 9 6 2   ◇ 10 8 7 4 3
♣ K Q 10 8 5 4   ♣ A 7

♠ A K Q 4
♡ K 8 2
◇ K J 5
♣ J 9 2

Even the experts are afflicted occasionally by the strange malady that we call bridge blindness. No doubt you have already spotted where South went astray. On the third club he should have discarded a heart from the table. It was clear that East was angling for a chance to over-ruff dummy, and there was no need for South to rely on West having either the jack of spades or the queen of hearts.

Whatever West returned at trick four, South could win, draw trumps, discard another heart from dummy on the third diamond and claim his ten tricks.

As is clear from the foregoing examples, it is mainly a matter of taking precautions in good time. The easier a problem seems to be, the more important it is to keep on the alert. After these words of caution, take over the play of the next hand.

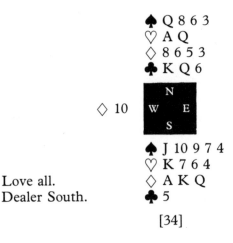

♠ Q 8 6 3
♡ A Q
◇ 8 6 5 3
♣ K Q 6

◇ 10

♠ J 10 9 7 4
♡ K 7 6 4
Love all.   ◇ A K Q
Dealer South.   ♣ 5

[34]

The contract is four spades. West leads the ten of diamonds and East follows with the two.

There are just three obvious losers in the black suits, but the risk is that the defenders may secure a diamond ruff as well. If the ten of diamonds is a singleton you are doomed, since East will surely have an entry in either trumps or clubs. What you must protect against is the combination of a 3–1 trump break and a 4–2 diamond break, two divisions that are highly probable.

There is more than one reason for leading a club at trick two. You cut enemy communication in the side suit, and you also establish at least one club trick. Here is the complete deal:

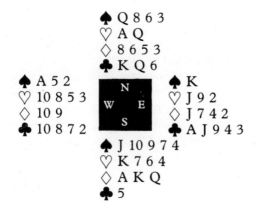

East captures the king of clubs with his ace and returns a diamond, to which West has to follow. You cross to dummy with the ace of hearts and hasten to discard your queen of diamonds on the queen of clubs. Now you play a trump, and when East comes in with the king his diamond return is harmless. You ruff high, and the only other trick for the defence is the ace of trumps.

Had you thoughtlessly played a trump at trick two you would have been defeated. East wins, returns a diamond, and subsequently regains the lead with the ace of clubs while his partner still has a small trump with which to ruff the third diamond.

```
                    ♠ 7 6 2
                    ♡ A 8
                    ◇ A 6 2
                    ♣ J 8 5 3 2
              ┌─────────────┐
              │      N      │
      ♡ K     │  W       E  │
              │      S      │
              └─────────────┘
                    ♠ A K Q 5 3
                    ♡ J 7
Game all.           ◇ K Q 8 4
Dealer South.       ♣ A 10
```

S	W	N	E
1 ♠	pass	2 ♠	pass
4 ♠	pass	pass	pass

West leads the heart king. What are your plans?

If the trumps are kind you will easily make your ten tricks. And a 4–1 trump break will not trouble you if the diamonds are 3–3. The most probable diamond split is 4–2, however.

The spectre that haunts you from the beginning is the possibility of 4–1 trumps and 4–2 diamonds. In this event you must aim to lose one trick in each suit except diamonds.

If your planning is sound you will let West win the first trick with his king of hearts. Your general strategy is to keep open the possibility of ruffing a diamond in dummy yourself while cutting the enemy communications. The precaution is necessary for the complete deal is:

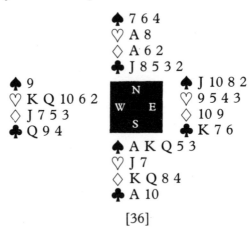

```
                    ♠ 7 6 4
                    ♡ A 8
                    ◇ A 6 2
                    ♣ J 8 5 3 2
    ♠ 9            ┌─────────────┐    ♠ J 10 8 2
    ♡ K Q 10 6 2   │      N      │    ♡ 9 5 4 3
    ◇ J 7 5 3      │  W       E  │    ◇ 10 9
    ♣ Q 9 4        │      S      │    ♣ K 7 6
                   └─────────────┘
                    ♠ A K Q 5 3
                    ♡ J 7
                    ◇ K Q 8 4
                    ♣ A 10
```

After winning the first trick West has nothing better to do than continue with a second heart. Dummy's ace wins and you test the trumps with the ace and king. As you feared, the division is 4–1. Now everything depends on avoiding a loser in diamonds. You cash the diamond king and continue with a diamond to the ace. When East follows all is well. You no longer have to rely on the 3–3 break. When you play the next diamond from the table East is caught in a dilemma. If he sacrifices his trump trick on your diamond loser, you can subsequently draw the remaining trump and claim ten tricks. If he discards, your queen wins and your fourth diamond is ruffed in dummy. Whether East ruffs or not, he can score no more than the one natural trump trick that is his due.

Note the importance of allowing West to win the first trick. If you take the ace of hearts at trick one and plan the play on the same lines, any East who is not completely asleep will defeat you by ruffing the third diamond, putting his partner in with the queen of hearts, and ruffing the fourth diamond with his remaining trump.

Securing Communications

Communication problems are constantly cropping up. This applies particularly at no trumps, where there are no ruffing entries to help in crossing to and fro between the two hands. Let us see from some examples how entry possibilities can best be exploited.

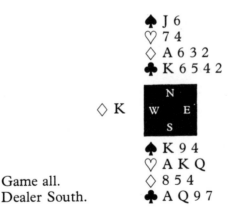

♠ J 6
♡ 7 4
◇ A 6 3 2
♣ K 6 5 4 2

◇ K

N
W   E
S

♠ K 9 4
♡ A K Q
◇ 8 5 4
♣ A Q 9 7

Game all.
Dealer South.

South opened one no trump, North gave a single raise and South closed the bidding with three no trumps. West led the king of diamonds. How would you have planned the play?

There are seven top tricks and it should be possible to make two extra tricks in clubs as long as the suit does not break 4–0. The snag is that the opponents have launched an attack on dummy's only side entry. The small clubs in your hand are high enough to block the suit. With clubs 3–1 and the diamond ace gone, you will be left with no way of reaching the established fifth club on the table.

A good rule is to render quickly unto Caesar that which is Caesar's. In bridge terms, if there is no special reason to the contrary, let the opponents have their tricks as early as possible. When you can keep the opponents off lead towards the end of the play, you have an extra measure of control and can steer the play in the desired direction without fear of hindrance. That is the commonest reason for giving the opponents their tricks at an early stage. Here you have something else in mind. Your intention is to overcome a blockage.

You allow West to win the first trick. If he switches, so much the better for that lets you keep the diamond ace as an entry to the fifth club. If West continues diamonds, you allow his queen to win the second round and his jack the third. Satisfied with three diamond tricks, West may now switch to hearts. Fine! Here is the complete deal:

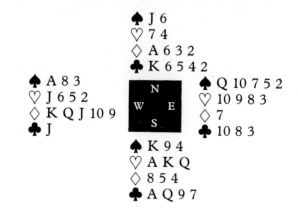

```
                    ♠ J 6
                    ♡ 7 4
                    ◇ A 6 3 2
                    ♣ K 6 5 4 2
  ♠ A 8 3                            ♠ Q 10 7 5 2
  ♡ J 6 5 2          N               ♡ 10 9 8 3
  ◇ K Q J 10 9    W     E            ◇ 7
  ♣ J                S               ♣ 10 8 3
                    ♠ K 9 4
                    ♡ A K Q
                    ◇ 8 5 4
                    ♣ A Q 9 7
```

You win the heart switch and play off the ace and queen of clubs. Had the suit broken 2–2 your precautions would have been unnecessary. When West shows out on the second club, you continue with a club to the king and play the diamond ace, discarding the blocking fourth club from your hand. After cashing the two clubs from the table, you have two further heart winners to bring your total up to nine tricks.

You appreciate, no doubt, that the game cannot be made except on this careful line of play.

Here is another three no trump contract.

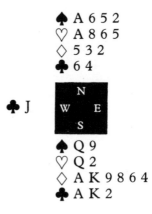

♠ A 6 5 2
♡ A 8 6 5
◇ 5 3 2
♣ 6 4

♣ J

♠ Q 9
♡ Q 2
◇ A K 9 8 6 4
♣ A K 2

West leads the jack of clubs and East follows with the eight. Your plan of play?

When the hand came up in practical play South saw no problem. He won the ace of clubs and laid down the ace of diamonds. He didn't like it one bit when West discarded a low heart, but he could do no better than continue with a small diamond. East's return of the queen of clubs was allowed to win. South had to take the next club, and the play of the king and another diamond put East on lead again.

If East had held the kings in both majors he could not have prevented South from gaining the lead to score the rest of the diamonds. However, the complete deal was as follows:

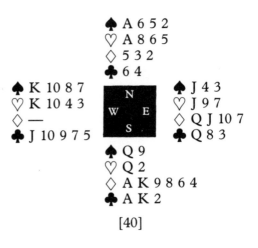

♠ A 6 5 2
♡ A 8 6 5
◇ 5 3 2
♣ 6 4

♠ K 10 8 7
♡ K 10 4 3
◇ —
♣ J 10 9 7 5

♠ J 4 3
♡ J 9 7
◇ Q J 10 7
♣ Q 8 3

♠ Q 9
♡ Q 2
◇ A K 9 8 6 4
♣ A K 2

When East returned a spade South took his chance by playing the queen. West's king forced out dummy's ace, and in the continuation South could make only the ace of hearts. Three down.

It seems doubtful if South had a plan of play at all. If he had counted his winners he would have realised that he did not need six diamond tricks, only five. There is nothing to be done if East is void in the suit, but South can guard against a void in the West hand. After winning the first trick he should play the nine of diamonds from hand. If both defenders follow there is no further problem. In the actual case the bad break is revealed, and it is a simple matter to make use of dummy's aces as entries and finesse twice against East's diamond holding to score nine tricks.

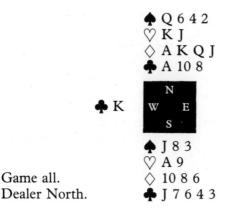

♠ Q 6 4 2
♡ K J
◇ A K Q J
♣ A 10 8

♣ K

♠ J 8 3
♡ A 9
◇ 10 8 6
♣ J 7 6 4 3

Game all.
Dealer North.

North opened one diamond, and with no interference from the opponents South became declarer in three no trumps. West led the king of clubs, dummy's ace winning the trick as East discarded the six of hearts. How would you plan the play?

In practice South counted seven top tricks and realised that he could easily establish an extra trick in clubs. Not much could be accomplished in spades since the honours were likely to be divided between the two defenders. Still, one never knew.

South's chosen line of play was to continue with the ten of clubs at trick two. The complete deal was as follows:

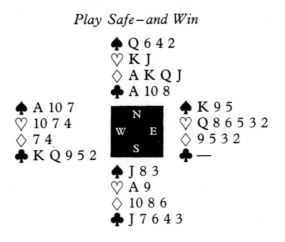

♠ Q 6 4 2
♡ K J
♢ A K Q J
♣ A 10 8

♠ A 10 7   ♠ K 9 5
♡ 10 7 4   ♡ Q 8 6 5 3 2
♢ 7 4   ♢ 9 5 3 2
♣ K Q 9 5 2   ♣ —

♠ J 8 3
♡ A 9
♢ 10 8 6
♣ J 7 6 4 3

East discarded a diamond and West allowed the ten of clubs to win. South cashed dummy's four diamond tricks, on which West discarded a club and a heart. Now South might have succeeded by the double-dummy play of the queen of spades. When in practice he played a low spade to his jack the result was one down.

South's decisive mistake came earlier. Do you see how he could have made sure of his contract?

There is a shortage of entries to the South hand, but declarer can overcome the deficiency by playing the eight of clubs at trick two and offering the trick to West. If West wins with the nine, South can subsequently overtake the ten of clubs with his jack and force out the queen. South thus makes two extra tricks in the suit no matter how West plays. It does not help West to refuse to win the eight of clubs. In that event South continues with the ten of clubs, establishing the jack as his ninth trick while he still retains the ace of hearts as an entry.

The majority of West players would have captured the ten of clubs at trick two, mind you, in which case South would have had no problem. But it does no harm to protect yourself against the possibility of running up against a hot defence.

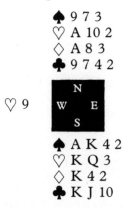

♠ 9 7 3
♡ A 10 2
◇ A 8 3
♣ 9 7 4 2

♡ 9

♠ A K 4 2
♡ K Q 3
◇ K 4 2
♣ K J 10

Love all.
Dealer South.

Against silent opponents South became declarer in three no trumps. West led the nine of hearts. What is your line of play?

There are seven top tricks, and if the queen of clubs is with East it will be a simple matter to gain the extra tricks that are needed by finessing twice. Thus reasoned South as he won the first trick with the ace of hearts and played a club for a finesse of the jack. West produced the queen and switched to the ten of diamonds. South won in hand and plugged away with the king of clubs. West promptly took the ace and played another diamond. South held up, but the defenders persisted to knock out the ace of diamonds, quite ruining the day for the greedy declarer. The complete deal:

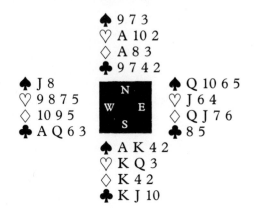

♠ 9 7 3
♡ A 10 2
◇ A 8 3
♣ 9 7 4 2

♠ J 8
♡ 9 8 7 5
◇ 10 9 5
♣ A Q 6 3

♠ Q 10 6 5
♡ J 6 4
◇ Q J 7 6
♣ 8 5

♠ A K 4 2
♡ K Q 3
◇ K 4 2
♣ K J 10

South was able to cash one club trick, but the nine of clubs remained in dummy like a stranded coconut. There was no way of coming to a ninth trick.

Perhaps South's hand was a little too strong. If he had held the queen of clubs instead of the king he would surely not have failed to make the game. Two club tricks are guaranteed if the suit is played from the top down, and the contract is lay-down as long as the temptation to finesse in clubs is resisted. The correct play is to put in the ten of hearts from dummy at trick one. If it wins, South has gained an extra entry to dummy and can afford to try a club finesse. When the ten of hearts is covered by the jack, South cannot afford the luxury of finessing. After winning the first trick he simply plays the club king. It makes no difference what the defenders do. South continues with the club jack when he regains the lead, and eventually plays the club ten. There is no way the defenders can prevent him from both establishing and cashing the club nine in dummy.

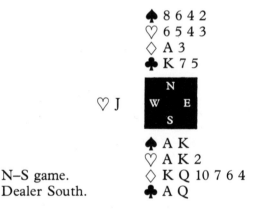

<pre>
                    ♠ 8 6 4 2
                    ♡ 6 5 4 3
                    ◇ A 3
                    ♣ K 7 5
                          N
          ♡ J   W   E
                          S
                    ♠ A K
                    ♡ A K 2
  N–S game.   ◇ K Q 10 7 6 4
  Dealer South.   ♣ A Q
</pre>

With no enemy interference South became declarer in six no trumps. West led the jack of hearts and East followed with the eight. How would you have planned the play?

Thirteen tricks looked within reach if the diamonds could be brought in without loss. After winning the first trick, South unblocked the ace and queen of clubs and crossed to dummy with the ace of diamonds. The two of hearts was discarded on the king of clubs, and so far all had gone well. The fly in the ointment appeared when East was unable to follow to the second round of diamonds. The complete deal:

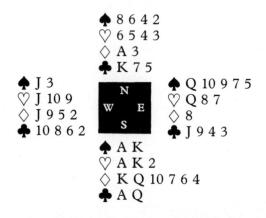

♠ 8 6 4 2
♥ 6 5 4 3
♦ A 3
♣ K 7 5

♠ J 3
♥ J 10 9
♦ J 9 5 2
♣ 10 8 6 2

♠ Q 10 9 7 5
♥ Q 8 7
♦ 8
♣ J 9 4 3

♠ A K
♥ A K 2
♦ K Q 10 7 6 4
♣ A Q

Sooner or later South had to concede a diamond to West, who promptly cashed a club to put the contract one down.

South was a little unlucky with the distribution. Five cards divide 3–2 in 68 deals out of 100, and in a further five or six cases the single diamond will be the jack. Nevertheless, South played in a foolhardy manner and did not deserve success.

The skilful card-player is a born pessimist. If you had been declarer you would naturally have handled matters differently. Realising that you had contracted for twelve tricks and not thirteen, you would have seen the danger of a 4–1 diamond break. You would also have remembered the good advice about Caesar. After winning the first trick and unblocking the ace and queen of clubs, you would have continued with a low diamond from both hands. When neither defender shows out, twelve tricks are there for the taking. The clubs are still under control, you have the diamond ace in dummy as entry to the king of clubs, and the long diamonds are now established. Giving up the possibility of an overtrick is a cheap premium to pay for insuring the success of a vulnerable small slam.

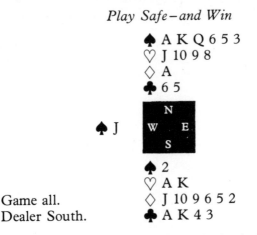

♠ A K Q 6 5 3
♡ J 10 9 8
◇ A
♣ 6 5

♠ J

♠ 2
♡ A K

Game all.
Dealer South.

◇ J 10 9 6 5 2
♣ A K 4 3

You play in three no trumps on the lead of the spade jack. The ace wins and your eyebrows shoot up when East discards a heart. How do you continue?

In practice South decided to establish his diamonds. He unblocked the diamond ace and played a heart to his hand, leaving the spade honours in dummy to stop the suit. On the second round of diamonds West discarded a spade while East captured the jack with his queen. South won the club return with the ace and played the ten of diamonds. East won the king and his club return knocked out South's last stopper in the suit. With the diamonds lying so badly, South had only one extra trick in the suit. On the nine of diamonds West discarded the club queen. The complete deal:

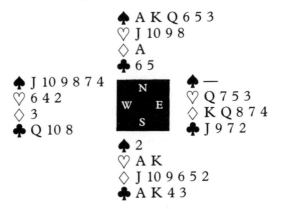

♠ A K Q 6 5 3
♡ J 10 9 8
◇ A
♣ 6 5

♠ J 10 9 8 7 4
♡ 6 4 2
◇ 3
♣ Q 10 8

♠ —
♡ Q 7 5 3
◇ K Q 8 7 4
♣ J 9 7 2

♠ 2
♡ A K
◇ J 10 9 6 5 2
♣ A K 4 3

The end of the story is that East defeated the contract with three diamond tricks and two clubs.

If South had known that West had no diamond entry, he might have succeeded by cashing three spade tricks before tackling the diamonds. Still, that would have been bad play.

Communications between the two hands are in a poor state although there are eight top tricks. If South's heart honours were not in the way, the ninth trick could be established by conceding a trick to the queen of hearts. But the blockage can be cleared away simply by playing three rounds of spades. This sets up three spade tricks for West, but no matter. Even if he has the queen of hearts as well it is not enough to defeat the contract.

South therefore makes a certainty of his game by discarding his high hearts on dummy's spade honours and then playing the jack of hearts to force out the queen. No matter what the opponents do, the ace of diamonds gives entry to the heart winners and nine tricks are made.

Communications can be troublesome in suit contracts as well.

```
                      ♠ Q J 5 4
                      ♡ 5
                      ◇ 8 7 5 4
                      ♣ K 6 4 3
                          N
             ◇ K     W       E
                          S
                      ♠ A K
                      ♡ A K J 10 8 7 2
E–W game.            ◇ 10
Dealer West.         ♣ J 5 2
```

W	N	E	S
1 ◇	pass	1 ♠	4 ♡
pass	pass	pass	

West begins with the king and ace of diamonds, East contributing the queen of diamonds and the two of spades. How do you plan the play?

[47]

If West has the ace of clubs you need lose no more than two tricks in the minors, for you will be able to discard one of your losing clubs on a spade from dummy. But can West have the ace of clubs? What can East have for his bid?

Meanwhile you have to ruff the second trick and tackle the trumps. When you have a particularly strong trump holding it is a good rule not to ruff automatically with your lowest trump. Make it a habit to ruff instead with a "middle-sized" trump. The thought behind the action is that the lowest trump may conceivably have some value in the later play.

The advice is applicable here, so you ruff the second diamond not with the two of hearts but with the seven or eight. When you test the trumps with the ace you have the pleasure of seeing the queen drop from West. How do your thoughts run now?

There is no need to lose a trump trick, but if the club ace is with East there is a risk of losing three clubs in addition to the diamond you have already lost. Is there any way to guarantee the loss of only two more tricks? Yes, with the help of a throw-in you can force East to give you access to the table. This is the distribution you have to guard against:

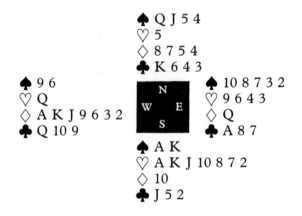

            ♠ Q J 5 4
            ♡ 5
            ◇ 8 7 5 4
            ♣ K 6 4 3

♠ 9 6   ♠ 10 8 7 3 2
♡ Q   ♡ 9 6 4 3
◇ A K J 9 6 3 2   ◇ Q
♣ Q 10 9   ♣ A 8 7

            ♠ A K
            ♡ A K J 10 8 7 2
            ◇ 10
            ♣ J 5 2

You continue with the king and jack of hearts, cash the ace and king of spades, and then throw East on lead with your handily-preserved two of hearts. The position is as follows:

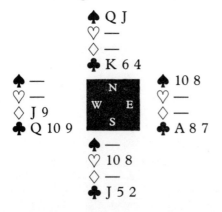

No matter what he does, East can make only the ace of clubs, Dummy's spades take care of your other losers.

Had you used the heart two for ruffing, East might have evaded the throw-in by playing his nine of hearts on an early trump. The contract would then have gone one down.

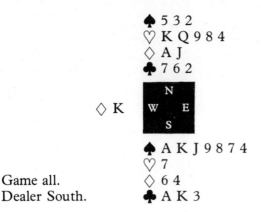

Game all.
Dealer South.

Without interference from the opponents you become declarer in four spades. West leads the king of diamonds. How do you plan the play?

If the trumps are 2–1 (the probability is as good as 78%) you have ten top tricks. And you will have no difficulty in organising an overtrick by knocking out the ace of hearts and using the five of spades as an entry to reach your heart trick.

It looked good, thought South as he won the ace of diamonds and continued with the two of spades to his ace. West discarded a diamond, for the complete deal was as follows:

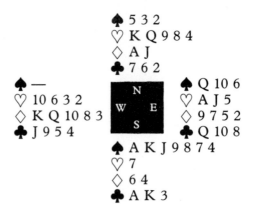

```
                  ♠ 5 3 2
                  ♡ K Q 9 8 4
                  ◇ A J
                  ♣ 7 6 2
  ♠ —                        ♠ Q 10 6
  ♡ 10 6 3 2      N          ♡ A J 5
  ◇ K Q 10 8 3  W   E        ◇ 9 7 5 2
  ♣ J 9 5 4       S          ♣ Q 10 8
                  ♠ A K J 9 8 7 4
                  ♡ 7
                  ◇ 6 4
                  ♣ A K 3
```

South played his singleton heart to dummy's king. East won the ace and returned a diamond to his partner's queen. A club switch came next, and South could do no better than cash the top clubs and get off lead with his small club. The trick was won by East who had a complete count of the hand. He returned a heart and South, with nothing but trumps left in his hand, had to ruff. There was no way of avoiding the loss of a trump to East, and that was one down.

South ought naturally to have asked himself if there was a way of overcoming the actual trump break. All three trumps with East has a probability of no less than 11%.

To begin with, West should be allowed to win the first diamond. If a switch comes at trick two, the diamond ace remains in dummy as an entry to the heart on which the club loser can eventually be discarded. No doubt West will continue with a second diamond to break communications. Now the two of spades is played, and the contract is guaranteed when East follows suit.

Just finesse the jack of spades. As the cards lie the finesse succeeds and, with no loser in trumps, you can afford to lose a trick in each of the other suits. If the spade finesse loses, you win the return, draw the remaining trump, knock out the ace of hearts, and later enter dummy with the five of spades to discard your club loser on the good heart.

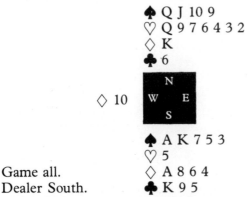

♠ Q J 10 9
♡ Q 9 7 6 4 3 2
♢ K
♣ 6

♢ 10

♠ A K 7 5 3
♡ 5
♢ A 8 6 4
♣ K 9 5

Game all.
Dealer South.

South opened one spade and North raised to four. West led the ten of diamonds to dummy's king. A friendly lead, thought South as he entered hand with the ace of spades and discarded the club loser on the diamond ace. A heart was conceded to East and the trump return was won on the table. South attempted to establish the hearts, but East had started with a singleton ace and South was held to nine tricks. The complete deal:

♠ Q J 10 9
♡ Q 9 7 6 4 3 2
♢ K
♣ 6

♠ 6   ♠ 8 4 2
♡ K J 10 8   ♡ A
♢ 10 9 7 5   ♢ Q J 3 2
♣ A 10 7 3   ♣ Q J 8 4 2

♠ A K 7 5 3
♡ 5
♢ A 8 6 4
♣ K 9 5

How many tricks can one win with an ace? Just one, obviously. In this example South can score one trick with the ace of diamonds, neither more nor less, whether he takes it early or late. If he is in a hurry it costs him a trump from each hand, which he can ill afford. To make ten tricks South must either establish the hearts, using dummy's trumps as entries, or cross-ruff to produce eight trump tricks, which, with the two diamond winners, will be enough for game.

After winning the first trick South should immediately play a heart from the table. East wins and plays the queen of clubs to the king and ace, and West returns his trump which is won in dummy. When East shows out on the next heart, South can either ruff two hearts high and concede a further heart to West, or cross-ruff to bring home his ten tricks.

♠ 10 6 3
♡ 8 2
◇ Q 6 5 4 3 2
♣ A J

◇ 9

```
        N
    W       E
        S
```

♠ Q 2
♡ A K J 6 3
◇ A K J 10
♣ 10 6

Game all.
Dealer South.

S	W	N	E
1 ♡	pass	1 NT	pass
3 ◇	pass	5 ♣	pass
5 ◇	pass	pass	pass

West leads the nine of diamonds and East follows with the seven. How should South plan the play?

At the table it went as follows. South won the first trick in his own hand and immediately drew the remaining trump. Then came the ace and king of hearts. When a third heart was ruffed in dummy, East showed out. South returned to hand with a trump and ruffed out West's queen of hearts. Now there was no quick way back to hand outside the trump suit. South tried a spade from the table. The complete deal:

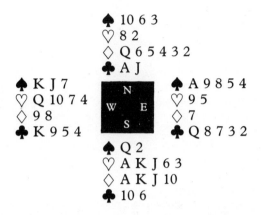

```
              ♠ 10 6 3
              ♡ 8 2
              ◇ Q 6 5 4 3 2
              ♣ A J
♠ K J 7            N        ♠ A 9 8 5 4
♡ Q 10 7 4   W        E    ♡ 9 5
◇ 9 8                      ◇ 7
♣ K 9 5 4         S        ♣ Q 8 7 3 2
              ♠ Q 2
              ♡ A K J 6 3
              ◇ A K J 10
              ♣ 10 6
```

East went up with the ace of spades and returned a club to the king and ace. In desperation, South entered hand with his trump and discarded dummy's club loser on the jack of hearts, but West won two further spade tricks to defeat the contract.

No doubt you will have spotted the mistake. South played down the game when he drew the outstanding trump at trick two. That was an extravagance he could not afford since he needed his trumps as entries. The right play is to start straight away on the hearts by cashing the ace and king. The third heart can be ruffed in dummy with the queen of diamonds. When the heart queen does not drop, South returns to hand with a trump and ruffs another heart. Now he can afford to enter hand with a third round of trumps, and the jack of clubs is discarded on the jack of hearts. South has a trump left to take care of the third round of spades, and the defenders can make no more than two spade tricks.

It looks risky to tackle the hearts before the last trump is drawn, but if the hearts are divided as badly as 5–1 and the queen does not drop there is never any chance of making the contract.

♠ A K 5 3
♡ Q J 10 9
◇ 4
♣ K Q J 2

♡ 3

♠ J 7
♡ A K 7 2
◇ A J 7 2
♣ A 7 3

Game all.
Dealer South.

S	W	N	E
1 NT	pass	2 ♣	pass
2 ♡	pass	4 NT	pass
5 ♣	pass	7 ♡	pass
pass	pass		

West led the three of hearts and East followed with the five. Should South try for ruffs in his own hand or in dummy?

There are seven top tricks in the side suits, which means that six tricks are needed from trumps. Two ruffs in one hand or the other will do.

It is customary, and often the simplest course, to go after ruffs in dummy. That is what South decided to do in this case. The nine of hearts won the first trick, and a diamond to the ace was followed by a diamond ruff. South returned to hand with the ace of clubs and ruffed another diamond on the table. He then led the queen of hearts, intending to overtake and draw trumps. But the bubble burst when East showed out on the second round of trumps. There was no way for South to recover. He was defeated for lack of an extra entry to his own hand.

South would have succeeded if he had tried for ruffs in his own hand. The difference is that dummy's trumps are solid enough to withstand a 4–1 break. But there is a small pitfall for the unwary. The hand illustrates the advantage of using the unsafe entries first and keeping the safe ones for later.

The complete deal was as follows:

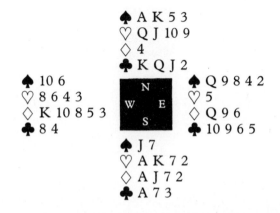

            ♠ A K 5 3
            ♡ Q J 10 9
            ◇ 4
            ♣ K Q J 2

♠ 10 6   ♠ Q 9 8 4 2
♡ 8 6 4 3   ♡ 5
◇ K 10 8 5 3   ◇ Q 9 6
♣ 8 4   ♣ 10 9 6 5

            ♠ J 7
            ♡ A K 7 2
            ◇ A J 7 2
            ♣ A 7 3

The right line of play, after winning the first trump in dummy, is to play off the ace and king of spades. The risk of finding spades 6–1 is not great—certainly much smaller than that of a 4–1 trump break. When the top spades stand up, the worst is over. South ruffs the third spade with the ace of hearts and West shows out. Now it would be easy enough for South to go wrong. It seems natural to return to dummy with a trump and ruff another spade according to programme, this time with the heart king. But to do so would be fatal on the actual lie of the cards. West has already discarded a club on the third round of spades, and he discards his last club on the fourth spade. When South subsequently tries to enter dummy with a club, West defeats the contract with a ruff.

Following the good advice at the top of this page, South should use the hazardous club entry to dummy at the earliest possible moment—immediately after the first spade ruff. At this point West has not yet had time to get rid of both his clubs. The safe trump entries to dummy can be used equally well in the later stages.

     ♥ Q

♠ A Q 8 5
♥ K 6
◇ 9
♣ Q 7 6 4 3 2

♠ K J 7 3 2
♥ A
◇ A 8 6 5 4
♣ A K

Game all.
Dealer North.

Again you are in a grand slam, seven spades this time. West leads the queen of hearts. How should you play?

There will be no problem if trumps are 2–2, or if they are 3–1 with clubs 3–2. Communications between the two hands are not ideal for coping with other distributions.

Murphy's Law tells us that if anything can go wrong it will, and you must look for a way of guarding against uneven breaks in both trumps and clubs. The declarer who played the hand neglected to do this. Winning the heart ace, he took out the ace and king of spades, West showed out on the second round. Now South needed the clubs to behave. All followed to the club ace but East ruffed the king to defeat the grand slam. The full deal:

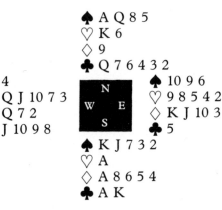

♠ A Q 8 5
♥ K 6
◇ 9
♣ Q 7 6 4 3 2

♠ 4
♥ Q J 10 7 3
◇ Q 7 2
♣ J 10 9 8

♠ 10 9 6
♥ 9 8 5 4 2
◇ K J 10 3
♣ 5

♠ K J 7 3 2
♥ A
◇ A 8 6 5 4
♣ A K

Do you see how South could have protected himself against 3–1 trumps and 4–1 clubs?

After winning the first trick South cashes the king of spades and the ace of clubs before crossing to the table with the spade ace. When the trump break is revealed, South cashes the king of hearts and discards the club king from his hand. He continues with a low club, and East cannot gain by ruffing with his remaining trump. South ruffs, draws the last trump with a spade to the queen, cashes the club queen and ruffs another club with his last trump. After the ace of diamonds, dummy is high.

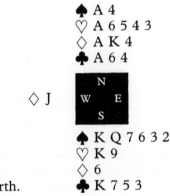

♠ A 4
♡ A 6 5 4 3
◇ A K 4
♣ A 6 4

◇ J

♠ K Q 7 6 3 2
♡ K 9
◇ 6
♣ K 7 5 3

Game all.
Dealer North.

Without interference from East and West, South becomes declarer in a contract of six spades. West leads the jack of diamonds. What is the safest way to play for the small slam?

A 3–2 trump break gives South twelve top tricks, while a 5–0 break leaves him with no chance. He should be all right if trumps are 4–1 and hearts 3–3. But can the contract be made if trumps are 4–1 and hearts 4–2?

The deal comes from a rubber bridge game. South won the ace of diamonds and immediately played on hearts, ruffing the third round in hand. West over-ruffed and returned a diamond to dummy's king, South discarding a club. On the next play of a trump to the king, West showed out. The complete deal was as follows:

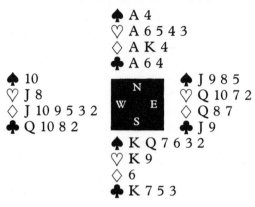

♠ A 4
♡ A 6 5 4 3
◇ A K 4
♣ A 6 4

♠ 10
♡ J 8
◇ J 10 9 5 3 2
♣ Q 10 8 2

♠ J 9 8 5
♡ Q 10 7 2
◇ Q 8 7
♣ J 9

♠ K Q 7 6 3 2
♡ K 9
◇ 6
♣ K 7 5 3

South was able to establish the fifth heart for a club discard, but there was no avoiding the loss of a trump trick to East.

No doubt you have spotted South's mistake. To avoid the risk of an over-ruff by the short trump hand, he should play a spade to his king at trick two. Then it is time enough to test the hearts. If he is over-ruffed on the third round of hearts, he must hope that West does not have the two remaining trumps. When he regains the lead he plays a spade to dummy's ace, hoping to extract West's last trump so that he can ruff a fourth heart without hindrance.

As the cards lie, West cannot interfere with South's first heart ruff. The trump position is revealed when a spade is played to the ace, and another heart is ruffed. South cashes the queen of spades and gives East his spade, which is the only trick for the defence. South's club losers are eventually discarded on the king of diamonds and the established fifth heart.

Retaining Trump Control

In a suit contract safety play is complicated by the need to avoid losing control of the trumps. If control is lost it may be hard or even impossible to make proper use of one's strength in the side suits. Here is a classic example of what it is all about.

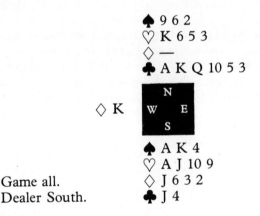

♠ 9 6 2
♡ K 6 5 3
♢ —
♣ A K Q 10 5 3

◇ K

♠ A K 4
♡ A J 10 9
♢ J 6 3 2
♣ J 4

Game all.
Dealer South.

South arrives at a contract of six hearts and West leads the king of diamonds. What is your plan of play?

There are eight tricks in the black suits and it is just a matter of clearing the trumps. You ruff the opening lead in dummy and play a small heart for a finesse of the jack. If the finesse loses you can cope with any return, drawing trumps and running the clubs to make your twelve tricks.

What if the heart finesse wins?

[59]

It appears to be a simple matter of crossing to the king of hearts, taking a further finesse against East if necessary, and drawing trumps to claim your small slam with an overtrick.

But it does not pay to trust your opponents any further than you have to. Be prepared at all times to find a snake in the long grass. The snake in question is revealed by a look at the complete deal:

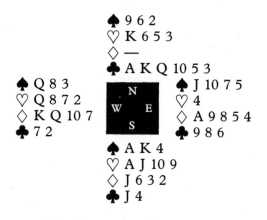

♠ 9 6 2
♡ K 6 5 3
◊ —
♣ A K Q 10 5 3

♠ Q 8 3
♡ Q 8 7 2
◊ K Q 10 7
♣ 7 2

♠ J 10 7 5
♡ 4
◊ A 9 8 5 4
♣ 9 8 6

♠ A K 4
♡ A J 10 9
◊ J 6 3 2
♣ J 4

West was quick-witted enough to hold up his queen of hearts. If you fall for the temptation of going back to dummy with the king of hearts, he will have succeeded in his wicked purpose. Control of the trumps will pass to West and you will be unable to make use of dummy's clubs. West will ruff the third club and return his remaining trump, leaving you with far too many losers.

West will derive neither pleasure nor profit from his deception if you are suspicious enough to foresee the possibility. The counter is a perfect safety play. After the successful heart finesse against East, you should now finesse against West, playing the ten of hearts and letting it run if West plays low. At all costs you must smoke out the queen of hearts so that you retain control of the trumps. If East scores an unnecessary trick with the heart queen, he is welcome to it, for the rest of the tricks are yours. The king of hearts in dummy can take care of a diamond return, and there is nothing the defenders can do.

As the cards lie your second heart finesse also wins as East shows out. It is then a simple matter to draw the rest of the trumps, and your safety play earns a bonus in the form of an overtrick.

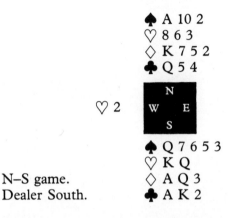

♠ A 10 2
♡ 8 6 3
◇ K 7 5 2
♣ Q 5 4

♡ 2

N
W   E
S

♠ Q 7 6 5 3
♡ K Q
◇ A Q 3
♣ A K 2

N–S game.
Dealer South.

You play in four spades on the lead of the two of hearts. East wins with the ace and returns the four of hearts, West following with the five. How do you play?

Having no further losers in the side suits, you can afford to lose two tricks in trumps. If the spades are 3–2 there will be no problem. If we took the spade suit in isolation at a no trump contract, it would be correct to start with the ace and then lead low towards dummy's ten on the second round. This method would ensure three spade tricks against any 4–1 break. It will not do here, however, for there is the threat of a heart force hanging over you. You must settle for guarding as far as you can against the possibility of a 4–1 break without thereby losing control of the trumps.

After winning the king of hearts at trick two, you should cross to dummy with the queen of clubs and play the two of spades. If East plays low you put in the queen. If the queen wins and West follows, you are home. If West has the king of spades, he does best to return a heart for you to ruff. Now you continue with a trump and finesse dummy's ten.

The complete deal:

[61]

```
                    ♠ A 10 2
                    ♡ 8 6 3
                    ◇ K 7 5 2
                    ♣ Q 5 4
    ♠ K J 9 8          N          ♠ 4
    ♡ 10 7 5 2                    ♡ A J 9 4
    ◇ 10 8        W       E       ◇ J 9 6 4
    ♣ J 8 3            S          ♣ 10 9 7 6
                    ♠ Q 7 6 5 3
                    ♡ K Q
                    ◇ A Q 3
                    ♣ A K 2
```

After winning the ten of spades you cash the ace. Then you play on the side suits and West may take his master trump whenever he pleases. The small trump in your hand takes care of the heart return, and you have nothing but high cards left.

The given line of play succeeds against all 4–1 spade breaks except singleton king with West.

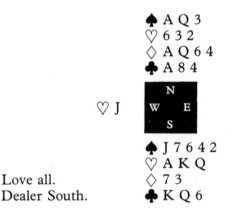

```
                    ♠ A Q 3
                    ♡ 6 3 2
                    ◇ A Q 6 4
                    ♣ A 8 4

                        N
        ♡ J         W       E
                        S

                    ♠ J 7 6 4 2
                    ♡ A K Q
Love all.           ◇ 7 3
Dealer South.       ♣ K Q 6
```

You play in six spades on the lead of the jack of hearts. East follows with the four of hearts. How do your thoughts run?

The spades can be brought in without loss only if you find West with the king and precisely one small spade. The slam will then be made even if you have to lose a diamond trick to East. If West has the king of diamonds, however, you will make the slam as long as you can avoid the loss of two trump tricks. The right method of handling the trumps is therefore dependent on the location of the diamond king.

After winning the first trick you should at once try the diamond finesse. If East produces the king, you must attempt to clear the spades without loss. You play a spade for a finesse of the queen, hoping to drop the king on the second round and to draw the remaining trump with your jack.

In practice the diamond finesse succeeds, for the complete deal is as follows:

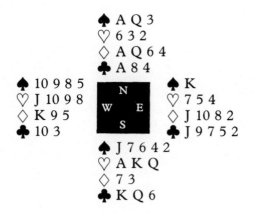

When the queen of diamonds wins you can afford to lose a trump trick. Since there will be no problem if the trumps are 3–2, you look for a way of protecting yourself against a 4–1 break, and you quickly realise that there are bound to be two losers if someone has a singleton, unless the singleton is the king.

The correct method of tackling the trump suit is to start with the ace. In this case your safety-play is well rewarded when the singleton king drops from the East hand. If both defenders had played small trumps under the ace you would have continued with the queen, and the slam would still have been safe on a 3–2 trump break.

Game all.
Dealer South.

The contract was four hearts and West led the ten of diamonds to the jack, queen and ace. You continued with the king of diamonds and a diamond ruff. Both defenders followed to the king of hearts but on the next round East discarded a club. You passed the trick to West who returned a spade. After cashing the top spades you ruffed a spade in hand, but West over-ruffed and played another diamond, East following. You ruffed the diamond and drew West's queen of hearts with the ace. Then you led the two of clubs, hoping that West would have to win and return the suit.

Should you have played the hand differently? Would it have helped if you had known that the complete deal was:

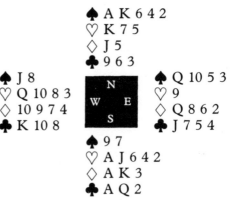

When you exited with the two of clubs East won with the jack and cashed the queen of spades to put you one down. As the cards lay, it would not have helped if you had tried the club finesse earlier.

You were a little unlucky with the lie of the cards but that was not the cause of your failure. You lost control of the trumps and were therefore unable to make use of dummy's spade length. You would have been all right on a normal 3–2 trump break, certainly, but you should have protected yourself as far as possible against a 4–1 division.

The right line of play is to establish dummy's spades. To avoid the hazard of a possible enemy over-ruff with a singleton trump, you cash the ace of hearts. Then you play on spades, ruffing the third round in hand. If the spades break evenly you need lose only two trump tricks. After cashing your second diamond trick you ruff your diamond loser in dummy and play an established spade, discarding the club two from hand. A defender is welcome to ruff if he pleases. You can win any return, cross to dummy with the heart king to extract the opponents' second last trump, and discard your queen of clubs on the fifth spade. Eleven tricks made.

On the actual deal West can over-ruff on the third round of spades, but it is immaterial how he continues. If he returns a diamond, you win with the king and play a trump to dummy's king. Now it need not worry you when East shows out. You offer West a further over-ruff by ruffing the fourth spade in hand. Whether he over-ruffs or not, he cannot prevent you from returning to dummy with a diamond ruff and discarding your two of clubs on the established fifth spade. By retaining control in trumps you limit the defenders to two tricks in hearts and one in clubs.

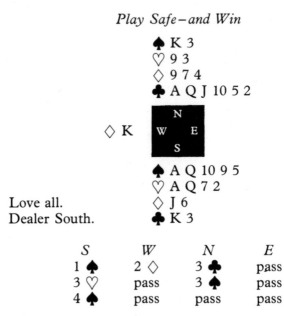

♠ K 3
♡ 9 3
◇ 9 7 4
♣ A Q J 10 5 2

◇ K

♠ A Q 10 9 5
♡ A Q 7 2
◇ J 6
♣ K 3

Love all.
Dealer South.

S	W	N	E
1 ♠	2 ◇	3 ♣	pass
3 ♡	pass	3 ♠	pass
4 ♠	pass	pass	pass

West starts with three high diamonds and East follows suit. You ruff the third diamond with the five of spades. How should you continue?

The six trumps that are outstanding will probably divide 4–2. If you play the trumps from the top, you will make the rest of the tricks when the division is 3–3 and also when the jack is doubleton. If the spades are not so kind this line of play will result in defeat. You might alternatively tackle the trumps by leading the nine to dummy's king and finessing the ten on the way back. This method will succeed when East has the jack of spades and one, two or three small cards in the suit. Is there any better possibility?

The problem really is to avoid losing control of the trumps. You have lost two tricks and can afford to lose one more. If you can just clear the trumps you will have more than enough tricks for your contract in clubs.

The right move is to play the nine or ten of spades and run it if West plays low. It doesn't matter if East scores a trick with the jack, for the spade king in dummy protects against a diamond force. The complete deal:

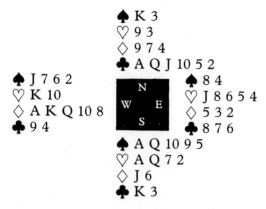

♠ K 3
♡ 9 3
♢ 9 7 4
♣ A Q J 10 5 2

♠ J 7 6 2
♡ K 10
♢ A K Q 10 8
♣ 9 4

♠ 8 4
♡ J 8 6 5 4
♢ 5 3 2
♣ 8 7 6

♠ A Q 10 9 5
♡ A Q 7 2
♢ J 6
♣ K 3

At the table South played top trumps. When East showed out on the third round, South had to try for as many club tricks as possible. West ruffed the third club and continued diamonds. Two off.

On correct play the first-round trump finesse succeeds. South cashes the spade king, returns to hand with the ace of hearts, draws trumps and makes an overtrick.

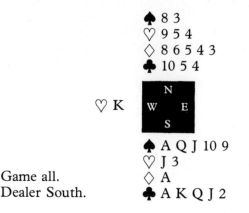

♠ 8 3
♡ 9 5 4
♢ 8 6 5 4 3
♣ 10 5 4

♡ K

♠ A Q J 10 9
♡ J 3
♢ A
♣ A K Q J 2

Game all.
Dealer South.

South began with a game force, North applied the brakes for all he was worth, and South eventually became declarer in four spades. West began with three rounds of hearts. How would you have planned the play?

At the table South ruffed the third heart with the nine of spades, crossed to dummy's ten of clubs, and took a successful trump finesse. Both defenders followed to the ace of spades, but when South continued with another spade West showed out. East took his king and continued with a heart, forcing out South's last trump and establishing a second trump trick for himself. One down.

The complete deal:

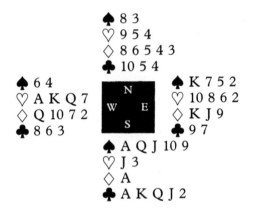

```
                    ♠ 8 3
                    ♡ 9 5 4
                    ◊ 8 6 5 4 3
                    ♣ 10 5 4
  ♠ 6 4                          ♠ K 7 5 2
  ♡ A K Q 7        N             ♡ 10 8 6 2
  ◊ Q 10 7 2    W     E          ◊ K J 9
  ♣ 8 6 3          S             ♣ 9 7
                    ♠ A Q J 10 9
                    ♡ J 3
                    ◊ A
                    ♣ A K Q J 2
```

South was defeated because he lost trump control. There were only seven trumps between the two hands to start with and the third round of hearts reduced them to six. A further heart force was imminent.

South needs to draw trumps before he can make use of the clubs. To avoid losing control, he should start with the spade queen from hand. If a defender wins with the king, the eight of spades in dummy protects against a further heart lead. East does best to hold up his king, but now South uses the ten of clubs as an entry to take a spade finesse. South doesn't mind losing to West if the trumps are 3–3. There is no chance if West started with the king and three small trumps, unless he is now out of hearts. It is the king and three small trumps with East that South is guarding against.

When the spade finesse succeeds, South continues with the ace of spades. The king does not fall, but now South simply plays on clubs, allowing East to take his master spade when he pleases. Correct play thus holds the defenders to two heart tricks and one trump.

It is worth nothing, however, that if West has king and another spade plus nerves of steel, he may lure South to his doom by playing low when the spade queen is led. Well, in that case West deserves his success.

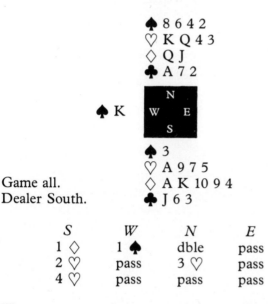

♠ 8 6 4 2
♡ K Q 4 3
◇ Q J
♣ A 7 2

♠ K

♠ 3
♡ A 9 7 5
◇ A K 10 9 4
♣ J 6 3

Game all.
Dealer South.

S	W	N	E
1 ◇	1 ♠	dble	pass
2 ♡	pass	3 ♡	pass
4 ♡	pass	pass	pass

West starts with the two top spades. Your line of play?

In practice South ruffed the second spade and played a low heart to the king. After ruffing another spade he cashed the ace of hearts, and the snag appeared when East discarded a club. South tried to recover by playing three rounds of diamonds, discarding the last spade from dummy. West ruffed the third diamond and played another spade. South ruffed in dummy and drew the last trump but, after cashing the ace of clubs, he had to concede the last two tricks for one down.

That was an inglorious end to the play in view of the good cards South held. True, he would have made twelve tricks on a 3–2 trump break. He should have reflected, however, that he had not bid a slam and that the full deal might be something like:

[69]

Play Safe – and Win

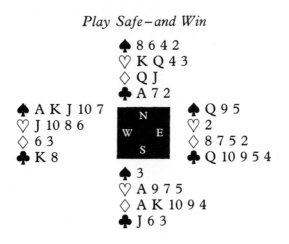

How could South have made sure of his contract?

It is just a matter of retaining trump control. After ruffing the second spade South plays a low trump from both hands. He gladly concedes this trick in order to guard against a 4–1 break. The small heart in the short trump hand takes care of any further spade lead. It is immaterial what the defenders do. South can arrange to ruff another spade himself to make eleven tricks.

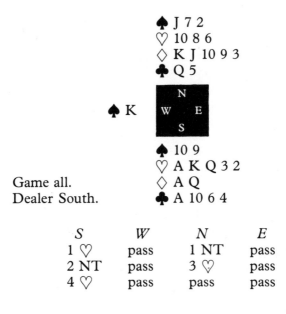

Game all.
Dealer South.

S	W	N	E
1 ♡	pass	1 NT	pass
2 NT	pass	3 ♡	pass
4 ♡	pass	pass	pass

The defenders started with three rounds of spades and South ruffed. He tested the trumps with the ace and king and was not at all pleased to discover that West had a singleton. It meant that East had a sure trump trick and there was nothing to be done about it. South drew a further trump with the queen and then started on the diamonds, overtaking the queen with dummy's king on the second round and continuing with a third diamond. East ruffed with the jack of hearts and returned a spade, which took out South's last trump. The complete deal was as follows:

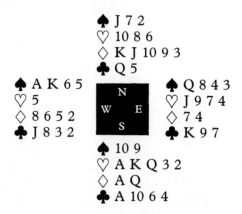

```
              ♠ J 7 2
              ♡ 10 8 6
              ◇ K J 10 9 3
              ♣ Q 5
♠ A K 6 5                      ♠ Q 8 4 3
♡ 5           N                ♡ J 9 7 4
◇ 8 6 5 2   W   E              ◇ 7 4
♣ J 8 3 2     S                ♣ K 9 7
              ♠ 10 9
              ♡ A K Q 3 2
              ◇ A Q
              ♣ A 10 6 4
```

South could have escaped for one off if he had allowed the fourth spade to win. East would then have been forced to lead a club away from his king. As it was, after ruffing the fourth spade South played a club towards dummy. The queen was captured by the king and South had to lose a further club for two down.

The play was faulty from the beginning. When South cashed the ace and king of hearts he lost control of the trump suit. He would certainly have made an overtrick if the trumps had been 3–2, but he should have concentrated on making sure of his contract. He can do this, once both defenders have followed to the ace of hearts, by continuing with a low heart from both hands. Dummy's third trump stands on guard against a further spade lead. No matter what the defenders return, South comes in, draws the remaining trumps and claims his contract.

Play Safe – and Win

```
             ♠ K J 5 3
             ♡ K 8 4
             ◇ 6 3 2
             ♣ J 6 2
                ┌─────────┐
                │    N    │
     ♣ K        │ W     E │
                │    S    │
                └─────────┘
             ♠ 7 2
             ♡ A Q J 10 3
             ◇ A K 9 7 4
             ♣ 9
```

Love all.
Dealer West.

W	N	E	S
pass	pass	pass	1 ♡
pass	1 ♠	pass	2 ◇
pass	2 ♡	pass	3 ♡
pass	4 ♡	pass	pass
pass			

West began with two top clubs. South ruffed and tested trumps with the queen and jack. When all followed, he cashed the top diamonds and conceded a diamond to establish the suit. West won with the jack and returned another club for South to ruff.

In tackling the spades, South reasoned that West, who had produced the ace and king of clubs and the diamond jack, would have opened the bidding if he had held the ace of spades as well. He therefore inserted the jack of spades from dummy. It was the right thing to do, for the complete hand was:

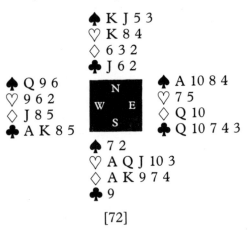

```
             ♠ K J 5 3
             ♡ K 8 4
             ◇ 6 3 2
             ♣ J 6 2
  ♠ Q 9 6        ┌─────────┐        ♠ A 10 8 4
  ♡ 9 6 2        │    N    │        ♡ 7 5
  ◇ J 8 5        │ W     E │        ◇ Q 10
  ♣ A K 8 5      │    S    │        ♣ Q 10 7 4 3
                 └─────────┘
             ♠ 7 2
             ♡ A Q J 10 3
             ◇ A K 9 7 4
             ♣ 9
```

[72]

The jack of spades was won by the ace, and South might have succeeded if a weaker player had been in the East seat. East found the right return, however, in this position:

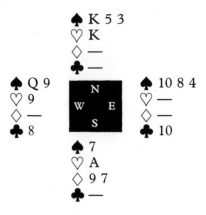

South had lost three tricks and it looked as though he would take the rest. But it didn't work out that way when East returned his club into the double void. South was without recourse. No matter where he ruffed, the defenders had to make another trick.

South cashed too many early winners. On the assumption that the spade queen is with West and that the red suits are friendly, he had only three losers. But he neglected to establish his side suit while he still had control of trumps. He should cash just one round of trumps before playing the ace, king and another diamond. Alternatively he can draw two rounds of trumps provided that his next move is to play a low diamond from both hands. In either case, South has an answer to anything the defenders may try. If a club comes back when the diamond is conceded and if East plays a fourth club into the double void after winning the ace of spades, South ruffs in dummy. The vital difference is that he has open communication in hearts or in diamonds and thus can return to hand to draw the last trump and enjoy the rest of the diamonds.

[73]

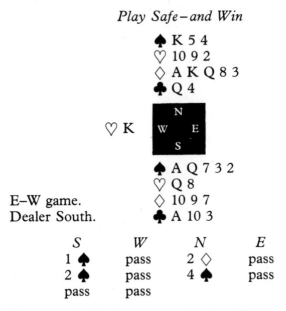

♥ K

♠ K 5 4
♡ 10 9 2
◇ A K Q 8 3
♣ Q 4

♠ A Q 7 3 2
♡ Q 8
◇ 10 9 7
♣ A 10 3

E–W game.
Dealer South.

S	*W*	*N*	*E*
1 ♠	pass	2 ◇	pass
2 ♠	pass	4 ♠	pass
pass	pass		

West attacked in hearts and South ruffed the third round. It would be an easy task to make eleven tricks if both spades and diamonds broke kindly. Anxious that no bad break should ruin his chances, South began with the ten of diamonds to dummy's ace. He returned to hand with a trump and continued with the nine of diamonds. If West had been void and had ruffed, both diamonds and trumps would then have been solid. West followed to the second diamond, however, and dummy's king was played. This gave East a bit of a problem for the complete deal was:

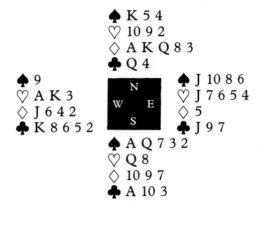

♠ K 5 4
♡ 10 9 2
◇ A K Q 8 3
♣ Q 4

♠ 9
♡ A K 3
◇ J 6 4 2
♣ K 8 6 5 2

♠ J 10 8 6
♡ J 7 6 5 4
◇ 5
♣ J 9 7

♠ A Q 7 3 2
♡ Q 8
◇ 10 9 7
♣ A 10 3

Not wishing to weaken his trump holding, East discarded a heart on the second diamond. South returned to hand with a trump, exposing the bad break, and now the far-sighted unblocking of the diamonds paid dividends. South was able to finesse dummy's eight of diamonds on the third round, leaving East helpless. If East ruffed, South would be able to draw the last trump with the king of spades and cash two more diamonds. When East refused to ruff, South simply continued with good diamonds from dummy and discarded his clubs.

```
                    ♠ 8 5 4 3 2
                    ♡ 6 4 3
                    ◇ 9 8
                    ♣ A 9 3
                         N
          ◇ Q     W         E
                         S
                    ♠ A 6
                    ♡ A K Q J 10
Game all.           ◇ K
Dealer South.       ♣ Q J 10 7 5
```

S	W	N	E
2 ♡	pass	2 NT	pass
3 ♣	pass	4 ♡	pass
pass	pass		

West led the queen of diamonds to his partner's ace. South ruffed the diamond continuation and tested trumps with the ace and king, learning that West had four and East a singleton. To avoid the impending diamond force, South switched to clubs, running the queen to East's king. East returned a club which West ruffed, and the trump return sealed South's fate. With no way of avoiding a spade loser, he had to go one down.

How would you have played it? The complete deal:

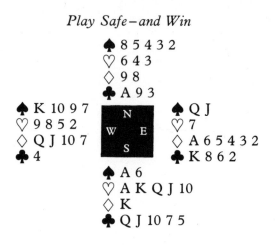

```
              ♠ 8 5 4 3 2
              ♡ 6 4 3
              ◇ 9 8
              ♣ A 9 3
♠ K 10 9 7         N          ♠ Q J
♡ 9 8 5 2      W       E      ♡ 7
◇ Q J 10 7        S          ◇ A 6 5 4 3 2
♣ 4                          ♣ K 8 6 2
              ♠ A 6
              ♡ A K Q J 10
              ◇ K
              ♣ Q J 10 7 5
```

South expired from self-inflicted wounds. Instead of ruffing the second diamond he should have discarded the losing spade from his hand. This retains trump control since dummy can take care of a third diamond lead.

South can cope with any defence. When West switches to his club at trick three, South goes up with dummy's ace, draws trumps, and concedes a third and last trick to the defence with the king of clubs.

```
              ♠ K 8 7 4 2
              ♡ K J 5
              ◇ A 6 3
              ♣ A 5
                   N
      ◇ 5       W       E
                   S
              ♠ Q 10 6 5
              ♡ A 9 3
N–S game.     ◇ J 2
Dealer East.  ♣ K 9 6 2
```

W	*N*	*E*	*S*
		1 ◇	pass
pass	dble	2 ◇	2 ♠
pass	4 ♠	pass	pass
pass			

The diamond lead was won in dummy and a low spade went to East's ace. East cashed the king of diamonds and continued with the queen. Determined not to allow an over-ruff, South ruffed with the queen of spades and West discarded a club. When South played a trump to dummy's king, East showed out, marking West with a sure trump trick. South had to fall back on a finesse of the jack of hearts, but the finesse lost and the contract was one down.

The complete deal:

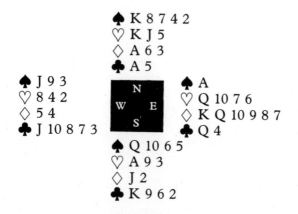

♠ K 8 7 4 2
♡ K J 5
◇ A 6 3
♣ A 5

♠ J 9 3
♡ 8 4 2
◇ 5 4
♣ J 10 8 7 3

♠ A
♡ Q 10 7 6
◇ K Q 10 9 8 7
♣ Q 4

♠ Q 10 6 5
♡ A 9 3
◇ J 2
♣ K 9 6 2

South needs to brush up his declarer play. From the bidding it was clear that East had a six-card diamond suit. South acknowledged that danger when he ruffed the third diamond high. But it was not a case for ruffing either high or low. South should have discarded a small heart on the third diamond, making use of elementary "loser-on-loser" technique. It is now immaterial how East continues. South has retained trump control and dummy can take care of a fourth diamond. As soon as South gains the lead he draws trumps and claims his ten tricks.

Shutting Out the Danger Hand

Safety play is often directed towards keeping the more dangerous opponent off lead.

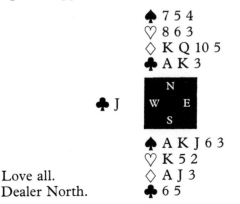

♠ 7 5 4
♡ 8 6 3
◇ K Q 10 5
♣ A K 3

♣ J

♠ A K J 6 3
♡ K 5 2
◇ A J 3
♣ 6 5

Love all.
Dealer North.

If you have landed in an optimistic six spades, you have not much choice in the play of the hand. Missing the ace of hearts, you cannot afford to lose a spade trick. The spades will need to be 3–2 and East will need to have both the spade queen and the heart ace.

There is more to think about if you were content to bid four spades. How do your thoughts run after the lead of the club jack?

One of your hearts can be discarded on the fourth diamond, but not until trumps have been drawn. Meanwhile it is dangerous to let in East, who may shoot through a heart to trap your king. You must do all you can to avoid the loss of a trump trick to East. You lead a trump from dummy and play low from hand if East plays the two. West presumably wins, but he can do no damage in hearts. Dummy wins the club return, and now you play a trump to your ace. It is as well that you took precautions, for the complete deal is:

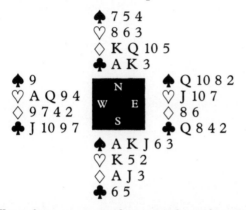

♠ 7 5 4
♥ 8 6 3
♦ K Q 10 5
♣ A K 3

♠ 9   ♠ Q 10 8 2
♥ A Q 9 4   ♥ J 10 7
♦ 9 7 4 2   ♦ 8 6
♣ J 10 9 7   ♣ Q 8 4 2

♠ A K J 6 3
♥ K 5 2
♦ A J 3
♣ 6 5

When West shows out on the second spade, you cross to dummy with a diamond and finesse against the spade queen. After drawing trumps you discard a heart on dummy's fourth diamond. Your only losers are two hearts and a spade.

If East puts in a higher trump on the first round, you play the ace, return to dummy in clubs, and play another trump. This time you cover East's card as cheaply as possible.

♠ 9 5
♥ 7 2
♦ 9 6 4 2
♣ K 8 7 6 2

♥ 3

♠ A K Q J 10
♥ A K 9
♦ K Q 5 3
♣ 4

Game all.
Dealer East.

W	N	E	S
		1 ♥	2 ♥
pass	3 ♣	pass	3 ♠
pass	4 ♠	pass	pass
pass			

[79]

West leads the three of hearts to the ten and ace. If the trumps do not lie too badly you should not need to lose more than three tricks in the minor suits. You can ruff the nine of hearts on the table and lead a diamond—East is sure to have the ace for his opening bid. What might upset your plans is a 4–1 diamond break, but there is nothing you can do about that. A pity there is only one entry to the table—the heart ruff.

At the table South cashed his top hearts and ruffed the third heart in dummy, West following. A diamond was returned and the king won the trick when East played low. Nothing wrong with the play so far. How would you continue?

South decided that his only chance was that East now held the ace of diamonds bare. He therefore continued with a low diamond from hand. The trick was won by West's jack, for the complete deal was as follows.

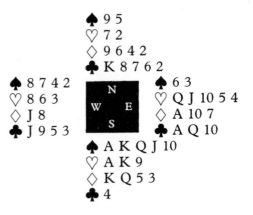

          ♠ 9 5
          ♡ 7 2
          ◇ 9 6 4 2
          ♣ K 8 7 6 2

♠ 8 7 4 2   ♠ 6 3
♡ 8 6 3   ♡ Q J 10 5 4
◇ J 8   ◇ A 10 7
♣ J 9 5 3   ♣ A Q 10

          ♠ A K Q J 10
          ♡ A K 9
          ◇ K Q 5 3
          ♣ 4

The play then developed unfavourably for declarer. West switched to the jack of clubs, which won the trick. South had to ruff the next club, and when he conceded a trick to the ace of diamonds East played the ace of clubs, forcing South to ruff yet again. This left West with a trump more than South in the following position:

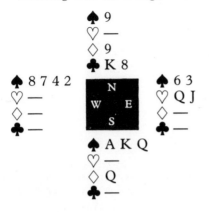

West could not be denied a trump trick and the contract was one down.

South neglected to keep the dangerous opponent off lead. The diamond ace is marked with East, and South is exposed to a force only if West gains the lead. South can prevent this by playing the queen of diamonds on the second round. East cannot profitably attack the clubs from his side of the table, and the nine of spades guards against a further heart lead. The best East can do is return a trump, and South gains a valuable tempo. Now he can afford to draw trumps and establish his tenth trick in diamonds.

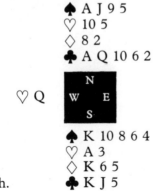

E–W game.
Dealer South.

South plays in four spades on the lead of the queen of hearts. How would you plan the play?

If you can find the queen of spades and draw trumps, you will have eleven easy tricks. And if the diamond ace is with East you will make a small slam. But what might the gremlins do to you? The defenders have developed a heart trick with their opening lead. If you fail to locate the queen of spades, a diamond may be led through your king and instead of making two overtricks you will be one down.

What you must do is keep East off play. The lead indicates that he has the king of hearts, but you can shut out that entry by allowing the queen of hearts to hold. You win the next heart, play a spade to the ace, and finesse in trumps on the way back. You have no interest in the rule of thumb that says you should play for the drop with nine trumps. The point is that you can afford to lose a trump trick to West but not to East. The finesse succeeds, for the complete deal is as follows:

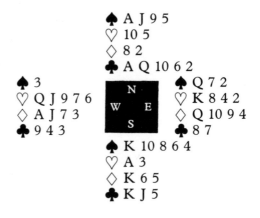

```
              ♠ A J 9 5
              ♡ 10 5
              ◇ 8 2
              ♣ A Q 10 6 2
  ♠ 3                          ♠ Q 7 2
  ♡ Q J 9 7 6      N           ♡ K 8 4 2
  ◇ A J 7 3     W     E        ◇ Q 10 9 4
  ♣ 9 4 3          S           ♣ 8 7
              ♠ K 10 8 6 4
              ♡ A 3
              ◇ K 6 5
              ♣ K J 5
```

Provided that you finesse in trumps against East, nothing can prevent you from making your game. When the finesse works you have eleven tricks.

If East had a singleton or void in trumps, you would simply concede a trump trick to West. With the king of diamonds protected you would still be safe for ten tricks.

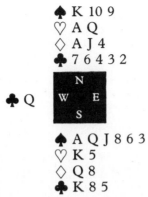

♠ K 10 9
♡ A Q
♢ A J 4
♣ 7 6 4 3 2

♠ A Q J 8 6 3
♡ K 5
♢ Q 8
♣ K 8 5

Game all.
Dealer South.

Three no trumps would have been an easy contract, but South landed in four spades and West led the queen of clubs. East won with the ace and returned the nine of clubs. How do your thoughts run?

At the table South put up the king of clubs and West ruffed. A diamond came back and declarer had no option but to try the finesse. East produced the king of diamonds and took the setting trick with the jack of clubs. The complete deal:

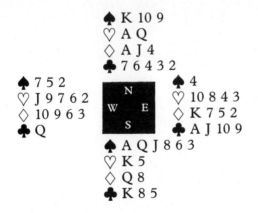

♠ K 10 9
♡ A Q
♢ A J 4
♣ 7 6 4 3 2

South missed the safe line of play. It looked as though West had led from queen-jack-ten in clubs and that East had ace-nine doubleton, but there was no need to take the risk of playing the king on the second round. .This was bound to jeopardise the contract if the queen of clubs happened to be a singleton. South can guarantee the contract by playing low on the second round of clubs. If West still wants to gain the lead for that awkward diamond switch, he has to ruff his partner's nine of clubs. Now South can make eleven tricks by playing the diamond ace, drawing trumps, and establishing the fifth club for a diamond discard.

If West allows the nine of clubs to win but ruffs the next club and switches to a diamond, South makes ten tricks in a similar manner, establishing the fifth club to take care of his diamond loser.

If it transpires that East has only two clubs after all, West may give his partner a third-round club ruff, but that is the end of the road for the defence.

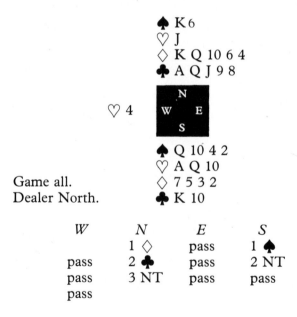

♠ K 6
♡ J
♢ K Q 10 6 4
♣ A Q J 9 8

♡ 4

♠ Q 10 4 2
♡ A Q 10
♢ 7 5 3 2
♣ K 10

Game all.
Dealer North.

W	N	E	S
	1 ♢	pass	1 ♠
pass	2 ♣	pass	2 NT
pass	3 NT	pass	pass
pass			

West led the four of hearts and East played the six under dummy's jack. How would you plan the play?

With two heart tricks and five clubs, South needs to develop just two tricks in the other suits. If the diamonds behave, eleven tricks will be there for the taking. There appears to be no problem.

At the table South overtook the jack of hearts with his queen in order to play a diamond towards dummy's king. East won with the ace and returned a heart. South tried the finesse of the ten, but West produced the king and continued the suit to knock out the ace. When South reverted to diamonds West discarded a spade. The complete deal:

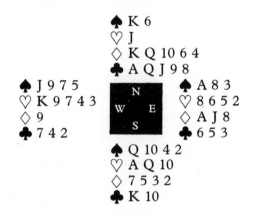

♠ K 6
♥ J
♦ K Q 10 6 4
♣ A Q J 9 8

♠ J 9 7 5   ♠ A 8 3
♥ K 9 7 4 3   ♥ 8 6 5 2
♦ 9   ♦ A J 8
♣ 7 4 2   ♣ 6 5 3

♠ Q 10 4 2
♥ A Q 10
♦ 7 5 3 2
♣ K 10

To avoid a large defeat South went up with the queen and ran his clubs. When he eventually played a spade from the table East rose with the ace and the defenders took the rest. One down.

Sloppy play resulted in the loss of an ice-cold game. South should have remembered the need to keep the dangerous opponent off lead. It cannot be right to give East an early chance to play a heart, and there is always that danger if the diamonds are attacked too soon. The right play is to win the first trick on the table and lead the six of spades. East can still gain the lead by playing the ace, but the difference is that this gives South the two extra tricks he needs for his contract. South can afford to concede the lead to East in these circumstances. If East plays low on the spade lead and the queen wins, South gains both a trick and a tempo and can immediately switch to diamonds to establish his ninth trick.

It would have made no difference if the spade ace had been with West. The hearts are then protected and South has time to develop his ninth trick in diamonds. No matter how the spades are distributed, the defenders can score no more than three tricks in the suit. South can well afford to lose three spades and the ace of diamonds.

```
                        ♠ K Q J 9 5
                        ♡ 5 3
                        ◇ K J
                        ♣ Q 6 4 2
                             N
              ♡ 4        W       E
                             S
                        ♠ 7 4
                        ♡ A Q 10
Game all.               ◇ A Q 10 6
Dealer South.           ♣ K J 5 3
```

S	W	N	E
1 NT	pass	3 ♠	pass
3 NT	pass	pass	pass

West led the four of hearts to the jack and queen. The spade suit seemed the most fruitful source of tricks, for even if it did not break 3–3 the ten might drop. South immediately led a spade to dummy's king. East produced the ace and shot back a heart. The finesse of the ten lost to the king, and West played another heart to knock out the ace. When South continued with spades, East proved to have a further guard in the suit. Since West held the ace of clubs as an entry to his long hearts, the result was one down.

The complete deal:

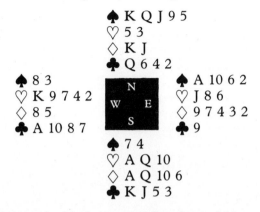

```
            ♠ K Q J 9 5
            ♡ 5 3
            ◇ K J
            ♣ Q 6 4 2
♠ 8 3              N              ♠ A 10 6 2
♡ K 9 7 4 2    W     E            ♡ J 8 6
◇ 8 5             S               ◇ 9 7 4 3 2
♣ A 10 8 7                        ♣ 9
            ♠ 7 4
            ♡ A Q 10
            ◇ A Q 10 6
            ♣ K J 5 3
```

Interchange the black aces and South would have made his contract. But he should have made it anyway by ensuring that East did not gain the lead until nine tricks had been established. The right play is a diamond to dummy at trick two and a low club back. If East has the ace and takes it, nine tricks are made without touching the spades. South has two hearts, four diamonds and three clubs. If the ace of clubs is with West, as in the actual case, no return is harmful. Only two club tricks can be developed as the cards lie, but South can set up two further tricks in spades to make his contract with an overtrick.

```
            ♠ 7 4
            ♡ A Q
            ◇ A J 9 5 4
            ♣ A J 10 2
                  N
    ♡ 7        W     E
                  S
            ♠ A J 9
            ♡ 10 6 4 2
            ◇ Q 8 7 3
            ♣ K Q
```

Game all.
Dealer South.

S	W	N	E
pass	pass	1 ◇	pass
2 NT	pass	3 NT	pass
pass	pass		

West led the seven of hearts and South tried a finesse of the queen. East produced the king and returned a low spade to dummy's weakness. South put in the nine, but West won with the ten and continued the suit. After holding up the ace of spades until the third round, South played a low diamond, intending to finesse dummy's jack. West was void in diamonds, however, and it was impossible to save the contract even though the spades were divided 4–4. The complete deal:

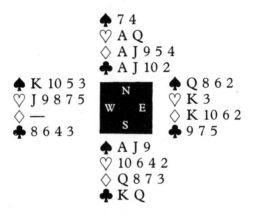

```
                    ♠ 7 4
                    ♡ A Q
                    ◇ A J 9 5 4
                    ♣ A J 10 2
    ♠ K 10 5 3         N          ♠ Q 8 6 2
    ♡ J 9 8 7 5     W     E       ♡ K 3
    ◇ —                S          ◇ K 10 6 2
    ♣ 8 6 4 3                     ♣ 9 7 5
                    ♠ A J 9
                    ♡ 10 6 4 2
                    ◇ Q 8 7 3
                    ♣ K Q
```

South should have planned his play better. He can make sure of the contract by rejecting the finesse of the queen of hearts at trick one. The danger of allowing East to gain the lead was obvious.

No matter how the hearts are divided the defenders can never make more than three tricks in the suit if South goes up with the ace. South continues with a club to his king and then plays a low diamond towards the table. If West follows with a low diamond, the jack is finessed, and eleven tricks roll in when West has the doubleton king or East the singleton ten. The overtricks are a mere side issue, however. On this line of play the game is guaranteed no matter how the enemy cards are distributed. In the actual case when West shows out on the first diamond, South can still bring in the suit for the loss of one trick. At worst the defenders may take three heart tricks, but as the cards lie they can score only one. The safety-play brings home the contract with an overtrick.

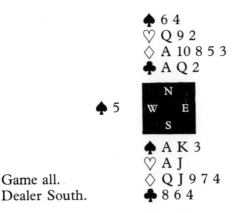

```
              ♠ 6 4
              ♡ Q 9 2
              ◇ A 10 8 5 3
              ♣ A Q 2
                    N
        ♠ 5    W        E
                    S
              ♠ A K 3
              ♡ A J
              ◇ Q J 9 7 4
              ♣ 8 6 4
```

Game all.
Dealer South.

Without interference from the opponents you become declarer in three no trumps. West leads the five of spades to his partner's queen. What is the safest way of playing for nine tricks?

If the diamond finesse is right there will be eight fast tricks and you can easily develop a ninth in hearts. There is a risk of defeat only if all three finesses are wrong. It will not do to allow the defenders to establish and cash their spades. This is the distribution you have to guard against:

```
                  ♠ 6 4
                  ♡ Q 9 2
                  ◇ A 10 8 5 3
                  ♣ A Q 2
  ♠ J 8 7 5 2           ♠ Q 10 9
  ♡ K 7 3        N      ♡ 10 8 6 5 4
  ◇ 6        W       E  ◇ K 2
  ♣ J 10 7 3     S      ♣ K 9 5
                  ♠ A K 3
                  ♡ A J
                  ◇ Q J 9 7 4
                  ♣ 8 6 4
```

It seems natural to start with a diamond finesse, but that will result in failure if the complete deal is as shown above. East will win with the king and knock out your second spade stopper, and when neither the club finesse nor the heart finesse succeeds you will be at least one down.

The right play, after ducking the first spade and winning the continuation, is to establish your second heart trick immediately by playing the jack from hand. This attacks the potential entry in the dangerous West hand before the spades have been set up. West wins and knocks out your remaining spade stopper, but now you are in a position to keep him off lead. You take the diamond finesse, not caring too much when it loses. If East has a spade left the defenders are welcome to another trick in the suit, for your nine tricks are secure.

If West switches to a club on winning the king of hearts, you take no chances but go up with the ace. You return to hand with the ace of hearts and take the diamond finesse as before. When East wins he cannot hurt you with any return.

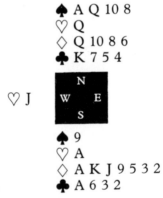

<table>
<tr><td></td><td>♠ A Q 10 8</td></tr>
<tr><td></td><td>♡ Q</td></tr>
<tr><td></td><td>◇ Q 10 8 6</td></tr>
<tr><td></td><td>♣ K 7 5 4</td></tr>
</table>

♡ J

♠ 9
♡ A
◇ A K J 9 5 3 2
♣ A 6 3 2

Game all.
Dealer South.

You land in six diamonds and West leads the jack of hearts. How can you make the best use of your resources?

If the clubs are 3–2 there is nothing much to think about. It is just a matter of drawing trumps and conceding a club trick. What you have to guard against is an unfriendly club break. Is it clear to you that the slam can be made against any defence and distribution?

After winning the first trick and drawing trumps, you play a club to the king and return a club to your ace. Someone must show out to create a problem.

If it is West who has the club length, your next move is to finesse the queen of spades. It makes no difference if the finesse loses. East, with no cards left in the minor suits, must either return a spade into dummy's tenace or lead a heart to concede a ruff and discard. Either way, both of your club losers disappear and you make the slam.

If East has the club length, he is the one who has to be kept off lead. You play the nine of spades to the ace and return the spade queen, discarding a club if East plays low. If West can win, he must concede your twelfth trick whether he returns a heart or a spade.

The actual deal:

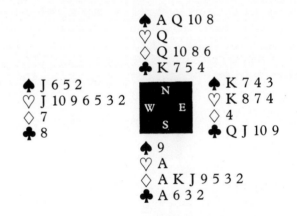

```
            ♠ A Q 10 8
            ♡ Q
            ◇ Q 10 8 6
            ♣ K 7 5 4
♠ J 6 5 2          N          ♠ K 7 4 3
♡ J 10 9 6 5 3 2           ♡ K 8 7 4
◇ 7         W       E      ◇ 4
♣ 8                S        ♣ Q J 10 9
            ♠ 9
            ♡ A
            ◇ A K J 9 5 3 2
            ♣ A 6 3 2
```

When East covers the queen of spades with his king, you ruff, return to dummy with a trump, and play another spade. The ten and the eight are now equals. When East plays low on the ten, you discard a club from hand. West wins with the jack, but the eight of spades in dummy takes care of your last club loser.

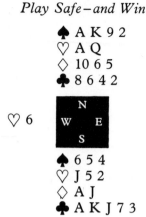

```
            ♠ A K 9 2
            ♡ A Q
            ◇ 10 6 5
            ♣ 8 6 4 2

      ♡ 6        N
              W       E
                  S

            ♠ 6 5 4
            ♡ J 5 2
            ◇ A J
            ♣ A K J 7 3
```

Game all.
Dealer South.

Against silent opponents you become declarer in three no trumps. West leads the six of hearts. How do you plan the play?

The declarer who had the problem at the table unwisely took the heart finesse. East produced the king of hearts and returned a diamond. West captured the jack with his queen, and low diamonds from both defenders on the second round took out South's ace. South crossed to the table with the ace of hearts and took a club finesse, but he was unable to make more than eight tricks when the complete deal turned out to be:

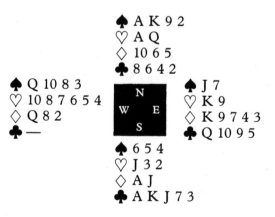

```
                  ♠ A K 9 2
                  ♡ A Q
                  ◇ 10 6 5
                  ♣ 8 6 4 2

  ♠ Q 10 8 3           N          ♠ J 7
  ♡ 10 8 7 6 5 4                  ♡ K 9
  ◇ Q 8 2          W       E      ◇ K 9 7 4 3
  ♣ —                  S          ♣ Q 10 9 5

                  ♠ 6 5 4
                  ♡ J 3 2
                  ◇ A J
                  ♣ A K J 7 3
```

South sowed the seeds of his own destruction at trick one, and East was sufficiently wide awake to find the correct switch to a diamond.

South should have realised the danger of allowing East to gain the lead at an early stage. The right play is to go up with the ace of hearts and play a club from the table, covering the card that East plays as cheaply as possible. South can afford to lose a club trick to West, who cannot profitably attack the diamonds. A further heart lead from West establishes the ninth trick.

On the actual hand this careful line of play produces five club tricks. There are four quick winners in the other suits, and it is a simple matter to establish a second heart trick to fulfil the contract with an overtrick.

```
            ♠ 10 8 6 3
            ♡ A K
            ◇ A K
            ♣ Q J 9 7 5
                    N
    ♠ J      W              E
                    S
            ♠ K 4
            ♡ 10 7 6 3
Love all.   ◇ Q 8 4
Dealer North. ♣ A 10 8 3
```

W	N	E	S
	1 ♣	1 ♠	1 NT
pass	3 NT	pass	pass
pass			

West led the jack of spades, East encouraged with the seven and South won with the king. Crossing to dummy with the ace of diamonds, South led the queen of clubs for a finesse. West produced the king and led another spade, and his partner took four spade tricks to defeat the contract.

It would be harsh to censure South too severely, for it is fatally easy to miss one's way in a position like this. It looks so obvious to win the king of spades at trick one, on the principle of now or never. The fact of the matter is, however, that South does not need a spade trick to make his game. The essential thing was to block the spade suit. East can be kept off lead in clubs, and even if the club king is badly placed South has his nine tricks. The right move is to play the four of spades at trick one. The complete deal:

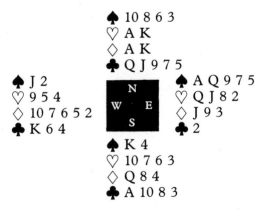

```
                ♠ 10 8 6 3
                ♡ A K
                ◇ A K
                ♣ Q J 9 7 5
  ♠ J 2                        ♠ A Q 9 7 5
  ♡ 9 5 4          N           ♡ Q J 8 2
  ◇ 10 7 6 5 2   W   E         ◇ J 9 3
  ♣ K 6 4          S           ♣ 2
                ♠ K 4
                ♡ 10 7 6 3
                ◇ Q 8 4
                ♣ A 10 8 3
```

After winning the jack of spades West can do no better than continue the suit. East wins with the ace and South's king falls. Dummy's ten of spades is now an effective guard, however, and the defensive communications in the suit have been cut. To avoid conceding a trick to the ten of spades East will probably switch to hearts. It makes no difference. Dummy wins and the club finesse is taken. The finesse loses, but South cannot be denied the nine tricks he has earned by careful play.

Blocking

The subject matter of this section has close links with what has gone before. We have seen a number of examples of how the success of the contract can be ensured by blocking the enemy suit. Usually the play is fairly obvious, but not in this case:

```
                    ♠ 10 7 2
                    ♡ 9 5
                    ◇ Q J 2
                    ♣ Q 10 9 8 2
                   ┌─────────┐
                   │    N    │
          ♠ 4      │ W     E │
                   │    S    │
                   └─────────┘
                    ♠ K 8 6 5
                    ♡ A K 10
Game all.           ◇ A K 8
Dealer South.       ♣ A J 6
```

S	W	N	E
2 ♣	pass	2 ◇	pass
2 NT	pass	3 NT	pass
pass	pass		

West leads the four of spades and East puts in the queen. What is your plan of play?

Clearly you must make use of dummy's club suit. Since the

[95]

probability is not great that East will have precisely king doubleton in clubs, it would not be a good idea to use dummy's only entry in diamonds in order to take a club finesse. There is too much risk of blocking the long club suit. No, you must develop the clubs from your own hand by playing the ace and then the jack. You can be sure of making four tricks in the suit which, with five top tricks in the red suits, will bring your tally up to nine. It follows that you need nothing from the spade suit. However tempting it may be to win the first trick, you should decline. If you capture the queen of spades with your king you will be defeated, for the complete deal is as follows:

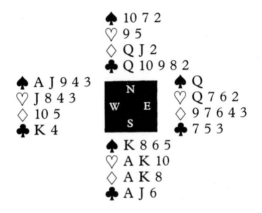

♠ 10 7 2
♡ 9 5
♢ Q J 2
♣ Q 10 9 8 2

♠ A J 9 4 3
♡ J 8 4 3
♢ 10 5
♣ K 4

♠ Q
♡ Q 7 6 2
♢ 9 7 6 4 3
♣ 7 5 3

♠ K 8 6 5
♡ A K 10
♢ A K 8
♣ A J 6

West gains the lead with the king of clubs and, if the king of spades has gone, he can cash four spade tricks to defeat the contract.

It is true that you are unlikely ever to make a spade trick if you refuse to take the king when you have the opportunity. But you have no need of a spade trick. And by holding up the king of spades you ensure the safety of the contract. If East continues spades, you will make your spade trick after all. More to the point, the defenders will make no more than three tricks in the suit—not enough to defeat you. As the cards lie, East has no spade to return and you are able to develop the clubs in peace.

On the next hand it is a matter of avoiding a blockage of your own.

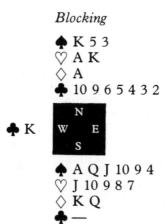

♠ K 5 3
♡ A K
◇ A
♣ 10 9 6 5 4 3 2

♠ A Q J 10 9 4
♡ J 10 9 8 7
◇ K Q
♣ —

E–W game.
Dealer North.

Without interference from the opponents you become declarer in a contract of six spades. West starts with the king of clubs. How do you plan the play?

At the table South ruffed the opening lead and tested the trumps with the ace. West showed out, discarding a heart. The complete deal was as follows:

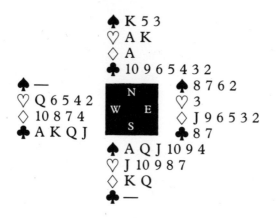

♠ K 5 3
♡ A K
◇ A
♣ 10 9 6 5 4 3 2

♠ —
♡ Q 6 5 4 2
◇ 10 8 7 4
♣ A K Q J

♠ 8 7 6 2
♡ 3
◇ J 9 6 5 3 2
♣ 8 7

♠ A Q J 10 9 4
♡ J 10 9 8 7
◇ K Q
♣ —

South left the trumps for the moment and played the ace and king of hearts. To his great disappointment East ruffed the second heart and returned a trump. South won in his own hand and continued with the jack of hearts, but West was not tempted to cover with the queen. He played low and South was finished. If he didn't ruff with the king of spades, East would ruff to defeat the contract. But if South did ruff this

[97]

trick in dummy, he would eventually have to lose a trick to the queen of hearts. South resigned gracefully.

When South learns at an early stage that the trumps are 4–0, he has reason to suspect that the hearts may also break badly. But this doesn't really affect the issue. No matter how the cards are distributed, the game is bomb-proof as long as South takes care to avoid a blockage. He has had to use one of his trumps to ruff the opening lead and he must draw four rounds to prevent East from ruffing. That leaves only one trump in South's hand, but it is enough.

Dummy has to follow to three rounds of trumps. On the fourth round the blocking ace of diamonds is discarded, clearing the way for South to cash his diamond honours. On the king and queen of diamonds the ace and king of hearts are thrown from the table. This in turn clears the way for South to lead hearts from his own hand. West's queen of hearts is forced out, and that is the only trick for the defence. South has the rest with the thirteenth trump and the established hearts.

Elimination

In suit play, and sometimes at no trumps as well, the safest plan may be to reject a finesse in favour of elimination and throw-in play.

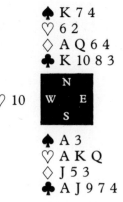

♠ K 7 4
♡ 6 2
◇ A Q 6 4
♣ K 10 8 3

♡ 10

♠ A 3
♡ A K Q
◇ J 5 3
♣ A J 9 7 4

N–S game.
Dealer South.

With no enemy bidding you become declarer in six clubs and West leads the ten of hearts. How do your thoughts run?

There will be no problem if you can bring in the trumps without loss, for you will then be able to afford to lose a diamond trick. Missing four trumps including the queen, it is mathematically correct to play for the drop. But on most hands there are other factors to take into account. You may have certain indications about the distribution, or it may be a matter of keeping a dangerous opponent off lead.

In this case we might put things the other way round. If you do not need to lose a diamond trick you can afford a trump

loser. A diamond must always be lost if the king is with East.
It may be helpful to discover at once where the king lies, so at
trick two you play a small diamond to dummy's queen. The
risk of a ruff is negligible since West did not lead the suit.

If the diamond finesse fails, you must subsequently hope to
be able to drop the queen of clubs in two rounds. If the
diamond finesse wins, however, you can adopt a line of play
that will be defeated only by a very malevolent lie of the cards.

The complete deal:

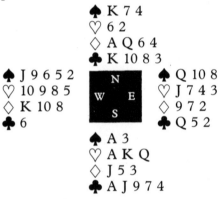

                    ♠ K 7 4
                    ♡ 6 2
                    ◇ A Q 6 4
                    ♣ K 10 8 3
    ♠ J 9 6 5 2   ♠ Q 10 8
    ♡ 10 9 8 5   ♡ J 7 4 3
    ◇ K 10 8   ◇ 9 7 2
    ♣ 6   ♣ Q 5 2
                    ♠ A 3
                    ♡ A K Q
                    ◇ J 5 3
                    ♣ A J 9 7 4

When the queen of diamonds wins, you cash your two
remaining hearts, discarding a small spade from dummy, and
play off the ace and king of spades, after which the elimination
is complete. With the odds in your favour, you have survived
the potential hazards of a 7–1 spade break or a 6–2 heart
break. At last it is time to play trumps. When both defenders
follow to the king of trumps you are home.

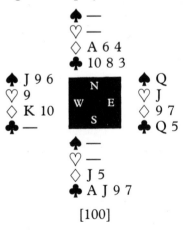

                    ♠ —
                    ♡ —
                    ◇ A 6 4
                    ♣ 10 8 3
    ♠ J 9 6   ♠ Q
    ♡ 9   ♡ J
    ◇ K 10   ◇ 9 7
    ♣ —   ♣ Q 5
                    ♠ —
                    ♡ —
                    ◇ J 5
                    ♣ A J 9 7

You play another trump from dummy and finesse when East plays low. As it happens the finesse succeeds and the queen falls under your ace on the next round. The defenders make one diamond trick but no more.

If West had been able to win the second round of clubs with the queen he would have been end-played, forced to yield your twelfth trick either by returning a diamond or by giving you a ruff and discard.

If East had shown out on the second trump, you would have played the ace and continued with a third trump to end-play West as before.

```
              ♠ 9 8 6 4 2
              ♡ Q 9 8
              ◇ A Q 9
              ♣ K 2
                   N
      ♣ Q     W         E
                   S
              ♠ A K Q 10
              ♡ A K 6
              ◇ 10 6 3 2
              ♣ 9 3
```

Game all.
Dealer South.

S	W	N	E
1 NT	pass	2 ♣	pass
2 ♠	pass	4 ♠	pass
pass	pass		

West leads the queen of clubs. How do you plan the play?

It looks like a certain game as long as the trumps are not 4–0. No human being leads the queen from ace-queen against a declarer who has opened one no trump. You must therefore reckon on two losers in clubs. If you are very unlucky East may have both diamond honours, giving you two losers in that suit as well. How can you make one of those four losers vanish? Yes, of course, with the help of a throw-in.

When the deal was actually played the distribution was as follows:

The club queen was covered by the king and ace. West won the club return and switched to a diamond, East winning with the jack when dummy played low. When South gained the lead, he drew trumps and tried the finesse of the diamond queen. East's king took the setting trick.

Naturally you don't play in that fashion for you have seen the need to protect against the unfriendly distribution. You allow the queen of clubs to win the first trick. Seeking to help his partner avoid the throw-in, West switches to a diamond at trick two. You reject the finesse and go up with the ace. After drawing trumps you cash your heart winners and then exit with the king of clubs. In with the ace, East must either play a diamond or offer you a ruff and discard. In either case one of your diamond losers disappears.

The play is just as easy if West continues with another club to his partner's ace at trick two. You win the trump or heart return, draw trumps and cash the hearts, ending in hand in the following position:

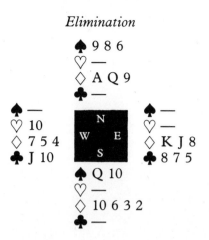

You play a diamond for a finesse of the nine. If West has both diamond honours you will make eleven tricks, but you are assured of ten tricks anyway since East has to concede the rest on his return.

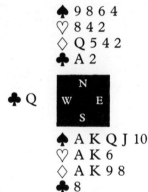

Game all.
Dealer South.

After an undisturbed bidding sequence South became declarer in six spades and West led the queen of clubs. Dummy's ace won and South immediately ruffed the two of clubs, thereby eliminating that suit. He continued with the ace of spades, both defenders following. How would you play from this point?

There is one heart loser, and the only danger is that the diamonds may break badly. If the suit is 3–2 or if someone has a singleton ten or jack there will be no problem.

Once the trumps are known to be no worse than 3–1, the

slam can be guaranteed. You draw trumps, cash the diamond ace and continue with three rounds of hearts. The complete deal:

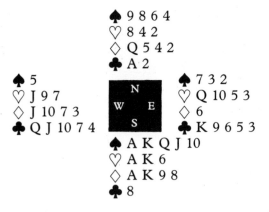

West's diamond holding is useless to him, for when he is forced to lead a diamond into the combined tenace he is unable to make a trick in the suit. Nor is it any better if he plays a club into the double void. Again South's diamond loser disappears.

South has to make his plan as soon as dummy goes down. The slam cannot be made unless the club is ruffed at trick two.

```
                    ♠ 10 8 6 2
                    ♡ Q 8 6
                    ◇ 7 5 4
                    ♣ A J 3
                        ┌───────┐
                        │   N   │
            ♡ K         │ W   E │
                        │   S   │
                        └───────┘
                    ♠ A K Q J 9 5
                    ♡ 7
Game all.           ◇ A Q 2
Dealer South.       ♣ K 6 4
```

S	W	N	E
1 ♠	2 ♡	2 ♠	pass
4 ♠	pass	pass	pass

West leads the king of hearts and switches to the ten of clubs. How do you plan the play?

West, who made a vulnerable overcall at the two-level, is pretty sure to have the king of diamonds. If it is doubleton you will not have to lose more than one trick in the suit, but you would rather not bank on that. West may have the queen of clubs, but it rather looks as though that card is with East. It seems likely that neither finesse is working, but fortunately a line of play that virtually guarantees the contract is available. Which line is that?

Play low from dummy on the ten of clubs, and play low from your hand as well if the queen does not appear.

The contract is now in danger only if West has led from a six-card club suit and can give his partner a ruff. This possibility is too remote to worry about.

After winning the ten of clubs West may continue as he pleases. Confident of success, he will no doubt play another club. The complete deal turns out to be:

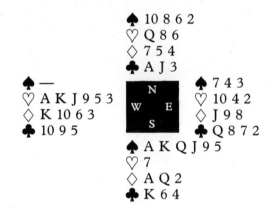

```
              ♠ 10 8 6 2
              ♡ Q 8 6
              ◇ 7 5 4
              ♣ A J 3
♠ —                          ♠ 7 4 3
♡ A K J 9 5 3   N            ♡ 10 4 2
◇ K 10 6 3    W   E          ◇ J 9 8
♣ 10 9 5        S            ♣ Q 8 7 2
              ♠ A K Q J 9 5
              ♡ 7
              ◇ A Q 2
              ♣ K 6 4
```

You win in your own hand, draw trumps with the ace, king and ten, ruff dummy's small heart and return to the table with the ace of clubs. The position now is:

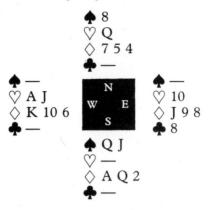

Knowing that West has the ace of hearts, you play the heart queen from dummy and discard the two of diamonds from your hand. The defence is helpless. On winning the ace of hearts, West must either return a diamond into your tenace or concede a ruff and discard.

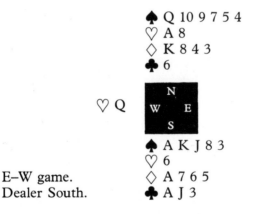

E–W game.
Dealer South.

With no opposition bidding you become declarer in six spades. West leads the queen of hearts. Can the slam be defeated if you play correctly? Only if one of the defenders is void in diamonds or has the singleton two.

There are no losers in any suit other than diamonds, and if

the diamonds are 3–2 there is no problem. Being accustomed to looking for gremlins, you consider how best to protect yourself against a 4–1 break. After winning the first trick with the ace of hearts, you draw trumps, cash the club ace, and cross-ruff clubs and hearts to eliminate these suits. Then it is time to tackle the diamonds. The complete deal:

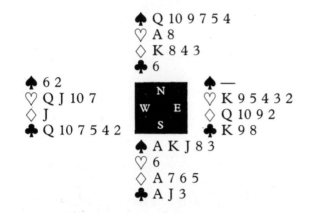

```
              ♠ Q 10 9 7 5 4
              ♡ A 8
              ◇ K 8 4 3
              ♣ 6
♠ 6 2                          ♠ —
♡ Q J 10 7        N           ♡ K 9 5 4 3 2
◇ J            W     E        ◇ Q 10 9 2
♣ Q 10 7 5 4 2    S           ♣ K 9 8
              ♠ A K J 8 3
              ♡ 6
              ◇ A 7 6 5
              ♣ A J 3
```

Let's go back and see what happened when the hand was actually played. After drawing trumps the declarer cashed the ace and king of diamonds only to be bitterly disappointed when West showed out on the second round. In a desperate attempt to save his slam, he ruffed the eight of hearts, cashed the ace of clubs and ruffed the club three in dummy, then returned to hand with a trump and played the jack of clubs which was covered by West with the queen. A diamond was thrown from dummy, and South would have been home if West had held both the king and the queen of clubs. West would have had to offer a ruff and discard on his return, permitting the last diamond to be thrown from the table. As the cards lay, of course, East won the trick with the king of clubs and cashed a diamond trick to put the slam one down.

You protected yourself against the unkind break in diamonds by going after an elimination from the start. When you had drawn trumps and eliminated the hearts and clubs, the lead was with dummy in the following position:

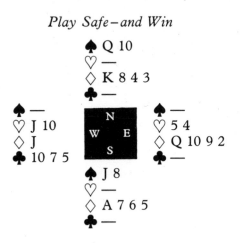

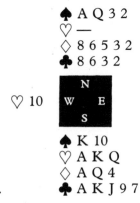

You continue by playing a low diamond from both hands. Either West wins the trick with his singleton jack, in which case he has to concede a ruff and discard on his return, or East goes up with the queen of diamonds to protect his partner from the fate. But East is in no better shape himself. To avoid conceding a ruff and discard he must return a diamond into your combined tenace, which allows you to score three diamond tricks.

The presence of several tenace holdings should always suggest the possibility of throw-in play.

Game all.
Dealer South.

After an undisturbed sequence South arrived in a contract

of six clubs. West led the ten of hearts and a diamond was discarded from the table. South took a normal view of the clubs when he played off the ace and king, but it transpired that East had the queen guarded. There was no way of avoiding the diamond finesse, and when that failed so did the slam.

Any comments?

South had two potential losers, one in diamonds and one in trumps. The four of diamonds would go on dummy's third spade. In fact it might be possible to discard two diamonds on dummy's spades if East had the spade jack.

With finessing possibilities in three suits, South should have chosen the elimination play which is safer than any finesse. After discarding a diamond from dummy on the ace of hearts at trick one, he should test clubs with the ace, cash the king of hearts for a second diamond discard, and then ruff the queen of hearts on the table. If all has gone well so far, prospects are excellent. The complete deal:

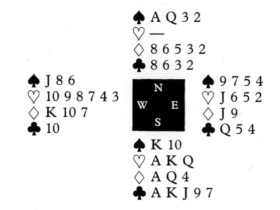

```
              ♠ A Q 3 2
              ♡ —
              ◇ 8 6 5 3 2
              ♣ 8 6 3 2
♠ J 8 6                        ♠ 9 7 5 4
♡ 10 9 8 7 4 3      N          ♡ J 6 5 2
◇ K 10 7        W     E        ◇ J 9
♣ 10              S            ♣ Q 5 4
              ♠ K 10
              ♡ A K Q
              ◇ A Q 4
              ♣ A K J 9 7
```

A trump is played from the table and the finesse is taken when East plays low. If the finesse succeeds, South draws trumps, discards his small diamond on the third spade, and tries the diamond finesse for an overtrick.

If the club finesse loses, West will have the choice of returning a spade or a diamond into one of South's tenaces or conceding a ruff and discard by returning a heart.

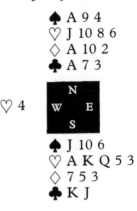

Game all.
Dealer South.

You arrive in four hearts instead of the lay-down three no trumps. West leads the four of hearts and East follows with the nine. How do you plan the play?

There are nine sure tricks and the tenth may come from a double finesse in spades—a 75% chance. A further chance is that the finesse of the club jack may succeed. Being a confirmed pessimist, however, you ask yourself if you can succeed when all three cards are wrong.

The answer is yes. West clearly does not have all three diamond honours or he would have led the suit, and as long as East has at least one of them your game is unassailable.

You draw trumps in three rounds, East discarding a club and a spade. Then you play a diamond towards the table, inserting the ten if West plays low. The complete deal:

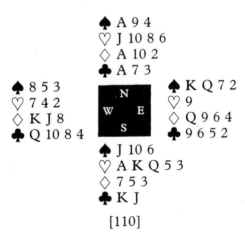

You don't want to let West in yet. If he plays the jack of diamonds you win with the ace and play three rounds of clubs, ruffing in hand. Then you play another diamond in this position:

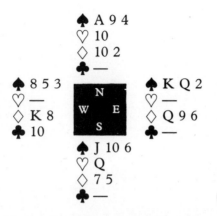

Now it doesn't matter who wins. If West goes up with the king and returns a spade, you allow East to win the trick. East can cash another diamond but must then return a spade into dummy's tenace or concede a ruff and discard.

The play develops in much the same way when West plays low on the first round of diamonds.

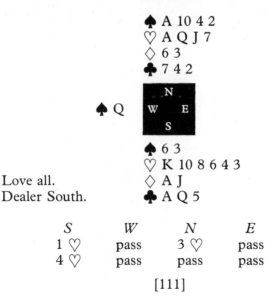

Once again, in spite of the good trumps, three no trumps would have been the best contract.

West led the queen of spades and the ace won. After two rounds of trumps, South led a diamond from dummy and put in the jack. West produced the queen and returned a spade to his partner's king. When a club came back, South had no option but to try the finesse. The queen lost to the king and the defenders could not be denied a further club as the setting trick.

South's line of play staked everything on the success of the club finesse. He should have made use of the help he received from the opening lead. As is so often the case, the contract was played down at trick one. The complete deal:

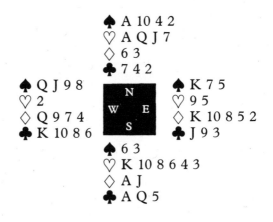

The first question an experienced declarer would ask himself on seeing that dummy is: "How can the club finesse be avoided?" The answer is the usual one: 'Elimination."

The lead of the queen of spades implies possession of the jack as well, and this can be turned to good account. It is undesirable to let East in to attack the clubs, but if a low spade is played from dummy at the first trick East cannot afford to play his king. That would permit South to score his tenth

trick by a later finesse against the jack of spades. So West wins
the first trick and can do no better than continue with another
spade. The ace wins and a diamond is played from dummy. In
accordance with his general plan for keeping East off lead,
South puts in the jack when East plays low. West wins with
the queen and, having nothing constructive to do, returns a
trump. The trick is won in dummy, the four of spades is
ruffed high, and the ace of diamonds is cashed. Dummy
regains the lead with a second round of trumps and the
position has become:

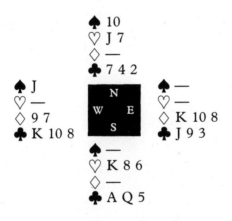

When the ten of spades is played and East shows out, South
discards the five of clubs from his hand. West is thrown in and
has to concede a tenth trick to declarer whether he returns a
diamond or a club.

The throw-in does not work if it is East rather than West
who has the spade length. If East follows to the fourth spade
South is obliged to ruff. He should then cash the ace of clubs
before crossing to dummy with a trump in order to lead
another club. If East plays low on the second club, South goes
up with the queen. He thus makes his contract whenever East
has the club king and also when West has the king doubleton.

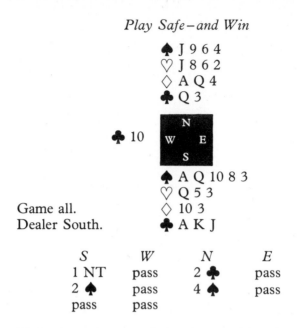

♠ J 9 6 4
♡ J 8 6 2
◇ A Q 4
♣ Q 3

♣ 10

♠ A Q 10 8 3
♡ Q 5 3
◇ 10 3
♣ A K J

Game all.
Dealer South.

S	W	N	E
1 NT	pass	2 ♣	pass
2 ♠	pass	4 ♠	pass
pass	pass		

To be dependent on a finesse is something the skilful player tries to avoid at all costs. Here it appears that either the spade king or the diamond king will need to be well placed. The two top hearts are missing and there is also a shortage of intermediate cards. It will be hard to avoid the loss of three heart tricks if you have to tackle the suit yourself. Even if the diamond finesse succeeds, the game will be by no means secure. The decisive factor is the spade finesse, which works when the complete deal is:

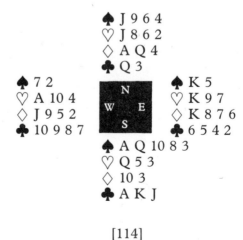

♠ J 9 6 4
♡ J 8 6 2
◇ A Q 4
♣ Q 3

♠ 7 2
♡ A 10 4
◇ J 9 5 2
♣ 10 9 8 7

♠ K 5
♡ K 9 7
◇ K 8 7 6
♣ 6 5 4 2

♠ A Q 10 8 3
♡ Q 5 3
◇ 10 3
♣ A K J

[114]

At the table South won the club lead in dummy and ran the nine of spades successfully. The king appeared on the second round of trumps and South won with the ace. Then he tried the diamonds, finessing dummy's queen. East took his king and returned a diamond, leaving South with the problem of the heart suit. On the lie of the cards there was no way of avoiding three heart losers and the contract went one down.

Once the spade finesse had succeeded, South could have guaranteed his contract irrespective of the location of the king of diamonds. The diamond finesse gains nothing even when it wins, for South has to tackle the hearts himself. The right play, after drawing trumps, is to cash the remaining club winners, discarding the four of diamonds from the table. The position is now as follows:

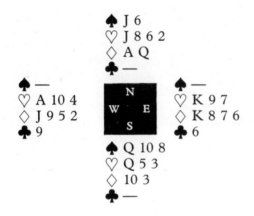

A diamond to the ace is followed by the queen of diamonds. It makes no difference which of the defenders comes in with the king. Whoever takes the trick has a choice between opening up the heart suit or conceding a ruff and discard, either of which gives South his tenth trick.

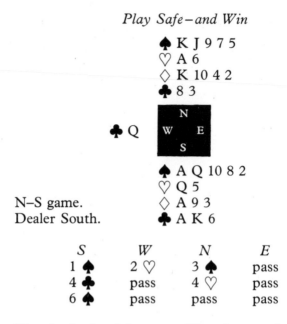

N–S game.
Dealer South.

S	W	N	E
1 ♠	2 ♡	3 ♠	pass
4 ♣	pass	4 ♡	pass
6 ♠	pass	pass	pass

West leads the club queen. How do you plan the play?

There is a loser in both red suits, but the chances of establishing the fourth diamond for a heart discard are good. If you play off the top diamonds you will succeed when the suit is 3–3 and also in the less favourable breaks when the honours are divided. Can you spot anything better?

At the table South found a variation, playing for an elimination and throw-in. It went well when the full deal turned out to be:

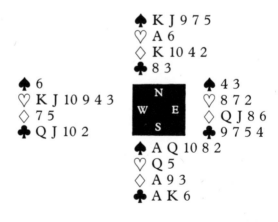

After winning the first trick with the ace of clubs, South drew trumps in two rounds. Then he cashed the ace and king of diamonds. As you can see, he would have been defeated if he had continued with a third diamond in an attempt to set up a further trick in the suit. After two rounds of diamonds, however, South cashed the king of clubs, ruffed his third club in dummy, cashed the ace of hearts, and continued with a second heart to the queen and king.

South reasoned that West, although short in trumps, could easily be short in diamonds as well. This was indeed the case, and after scoring the king of hearts West had to concede a ruff and discard. The elimination had worked.

South certainly made his slam but his line of play was not the best. You can no doubt improve on it.

West made an overcall at the two-level and there is not much he can have in the way of high cards. It is hardly possible that he does not have the king of hearts. And if he does have the heart king, the contract is unbeatable no matter how the other cards lie.

After drawing trumps and eliminating the clubs, you play the king of diamonds and continue with a small diamond from the table. When East plays low you insert the nine. On the actual lie of the cards, West is unable to beat the nine of diamonds and your slam is home. It would not have helped East to split his diamond honours. You would then have had no difficulty in establishing a twelfth trick in the suit.

Yes, but suppose West had been able to win the second diamond trick. It makes no difference. If West began with only two diamonds, he must now return a heart into your tenace or give you a ruff and discard. If West is able to return a diamond and East follows, the thirteenth diamond on the table will take care of your losing heart. Finally, if West started with Q J x x in diamonds, the position after his diamond return will be:

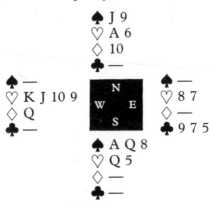

Now you have a squeeze in hand. On the run of the trumps West is unable to withstand the pressure in the red suits. Either the queen of hearts or the ten of diamonds will become your twelfth trick.

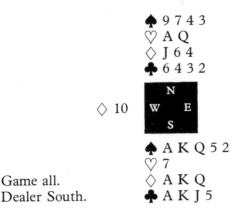

Game all.
Dealer South.

After an undisturbed auction South became declarer in a contract of six spades. West led the ten of diamonds.

It looked like an easy slam, but South was an experienced player and was not deceived by appearances. The diamond lead was won by the ace. South tested the trumps by cashing the ace and noted with relief that both defenders followed. Now it was just a matter of avoiding two club losers.

Since South was not in a grand slam, he concentrated in playing for twelve tricks in the safest possible way. Success

was guaranteed with the help of an elimination. The complete
deal was as follows:

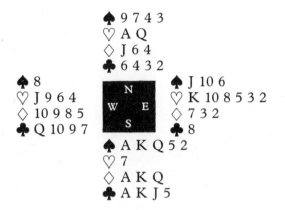

After drawing trumps, South cashed his diamond tricks
and eliminated the hearts with a ruff. He cashed the ace of
clubs but no queen fell. The ending was as follows:

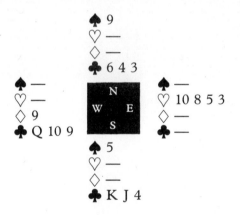

The elimination was complete and South led the four of
clubs from hand to effect the throw-in. No matter who won
the trick or how the cards were distributed, he was bound to
make the rest of the tricks.

Reserve-Trumps

We have already seen some examples of the use of a side suit as reserve-trumps when there is a weakness in the trump department. Let's have a look at a few more.

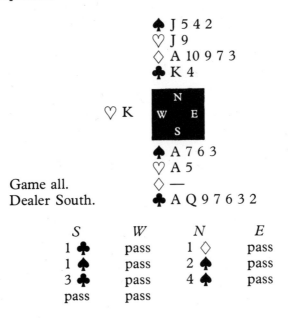

♠ J 5 4 2
♡ J 9
◇ A 10 9 7 3
♣ K 4

♡ K

♠ A 7 6 3
♡ A 5
◇ —
♣ A Q 9 7 6 3 2

Game all.
Dealer South.

S	W	N	E
1 ♣	pass	1 ◇	pass
1 ♠	pass	2 ♠	pass
3 ♣	pass	4 ♠	pass
pass	pass		

West leads the king of hearts. How do you plan the play?
At the table South won the ace of hearts, crossed to dummy with the king of clubs, and discarded his losing heart on the ace of diamonds. Then he played a spade to the ace and

continued with a second round of spades. It was swiftly brought home to him that he had not been so very clever, for the complete deal turned out to be:

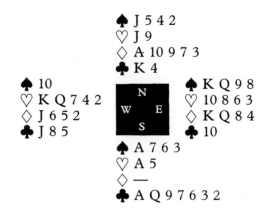

♠ J 5 4 2
♡ J 9
◇ A 10 9 7 3
♣ K 4

♠ 10
♡ K Q 7 4 2
◇ J 6 5 2
♣ J 8 5

♠ K Q 9 8
♡ 10 8 6 3
◇ K Q 8 4
♣ 10

♠ A 7 6 3
♡ A 5
◇ —
♣ A Q 9 7 6 3 2

To South's horror, East was able to draw trumps. West discarded his clubs and the defenders took the rest of the tricks. South made only one trick in each suit for a catastrophic result of six down.

The contract would have been made with an overtrick if the trumps had broken 3–2, but South should not have been concerned with overtricks.

South made two grave mistakes. He lost control of the trumps and he failed to make use of the clubs as reserve-trumps. The two mistakes did not cancel each other out in this case.

When the king of clubs stood up at trick two it was clear that the club suit would run. South discards the heart loser on the ace of diamonds and returns to hand with the ace of spades. When both defenders follow, the spades are known to be no worse than 4–1 and the contract is guaranteed. With no losers in the side suits, South can well afford to lose three trump tricks just as long as he keeps control of the situation. The right play is to revert to clubs, using the clubs as reserve-trumps. East can ruff when he pleases and return what he likes. South simply ruffs and continues with clubs. South has control and the defenders can make no more than their three trump tricks.

[121]

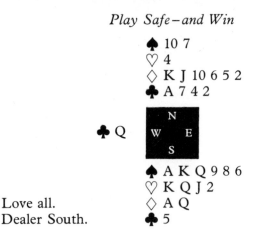

Love all.
Dealer South.

With no interference from the opponents you become declarer in six spades. West leads the queen of clubs.

On the club lead it looks like a grand slam. Just draw trumps and run the diamonds to notch up thirteen tricks. Gremlins? The trumps may lie badly. If West has the guarded jack of spades there is nothing to be done; you will have to lose the ace of hearts and a trump. A spade guard with East may be overcome with the help of an end-play. You need to shorten your trump holding and to use the diamonds as reserve-trumps.

Ruff a club at trick two and then play the king of hearts, establishing heart tricks in your hand and preparing a ruffing entry to the table. The complete deal:

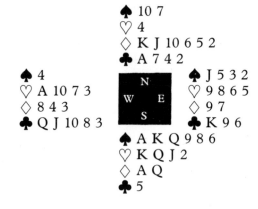

On winning the heart ace West can do no better than return a heart. You ruff in dummy and ruff another club in your hand. Now you are down to four trumps and it is time to find out whether your precautions were necessary or not. You test the trumps with the ace and king. If both defenders had been able to follow suit, all your pains would have been for nothing. When West shows out on the second trump, your foresight pays off. Now you are able to call upon your reserve-trumps. You cash the ace of diamonds and then overtake your queen with dummy's king. This is the position when you continue with high diamonds from the table:

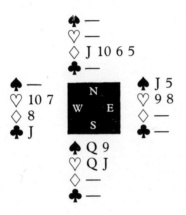

If East refuses to ruff, you discard both of your hearts. If he ruffs, you over-ruff, draw the last trump and cash your high hearts. East is bound to ruff eventually even if he waits until both of you have nothing but trumps left. Thus with the help of your reserve-trumps you are able to "finesse" against East's trump holding, but only because you took precaution from the start against a bad trump break.

It is a pity to lose control of trumps unnecessarily when the opponents launch a forcing attack. In most suit contracts it is a sound rule to set up a long side suit before tackling the trumps. In this way you retain control and have the option of using the side suits as reserve-trumps.

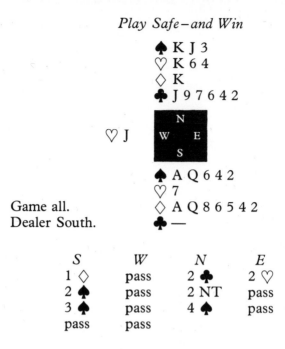

♥ J

Game all.
Dealer South.

S	W	N	E
1 ♦	pass	2 ♣	2 ♥
2 ♠	pass	2 NT	pass
3 ♠	pass	4 ♠	pass
pass	pass		

The jack of hearts was allowed to win the first trick. South ruffed the next heart, played a spade to the king and continued with the jack of spades, on which West discarded a club. South unblocked the king of diamonds before drawing the remaining trumps with the ace and queen. When he continued with a top diamond he was dismayed to find that West held the suit guarded. South could cash only the top diamonds and the contract was two down. The complete deal:

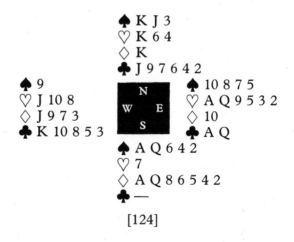

Would you have played as carelessly as South? No, of course, you would have observed the principle of establishing the side suit before drawing trumps. After ruffing the second heart you play a diamond to dummy's king and a trump back to your ace. When both opponents follow, you know that neither of your suits is breaking worse than 4–1. Correct play now makes a certainty of the contract.

No matter how the diamonds may lie, you make sure of establishing the suit by ruffing a low diamond on the table. And you are particularly careful to ruff, not with the jack of spades which could result in the loss of trump control, but with the king. Then you play the jack of spades and overtake in hand with your queen. This generosity results in establishing an extra trump trick for the defence, but you have no other safe means of access to the long diamonds. If the three remaining trumps are all in the one hand, you certainly cannot afford to return with a ruff. When West shows out on the second round of spades, you at least still have as many trumps left as East. Now you simply put the diamonds, your reserve-trumps, to work. So far you have lost only one trick. You can afford to lose two trump tricks to East, and nothing can prevent you from making the contract.

Cross-Ruff

When the intention is to play on cross-ruff lines, a routine safety measure is to cash the top tricks in the side suits as early as possible. Otherwise the opponents may discard while you are ruffing and eventually ruff your side-suit winners. It is not possible, unfortunately, to draw the opponents' trumps and still make your own trumps separately.

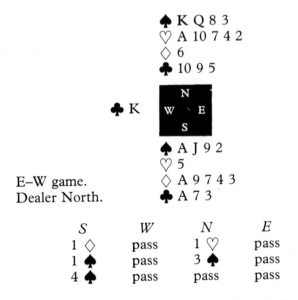

♠ K Q 8 3
♡ A 10 7 4 2
♢ 6
♣ 10 9 5

♣ K

♠ A J 9 2
♡ 5
♢ A 9 7 4 3
♣ A 7 3

E–W game.
Dealer North.

S	W	N	E
1 ♢	pass	1 ♡	pass
1 ♠	pass	3 ♠	pass
4 ♠	pass	pass	pass

West leads the king of clubs and East follows with the two. How do you plan the play?

You have no obvious suit to establish. There are three aces on the side but that is all. To make your game, therefore, you need seven tricks from the trumps—almost one trick for every trump you possess. With singletons opposite the aces in either hand it should go well. But it would be easy enough to slip up.

The ruffing is going to be done in the red suits, and if West had not started with a club you would nevertheless have cashed the club ace as soon as you could. Now you take the ace of clubs first. You play a heart to the ace and ruff a heart with the two of spades. Then you cash the diamond ace and ruff a diamond with the spade three. The risk of either suit breaking 6–1 is quite small, and anyway you have no choice in the matter.

When you continue with a heart for a further ruff, you should not take the slightest risk. Your sights should be set on just ten tricks, which you can make even though the cards are distributed as follows:

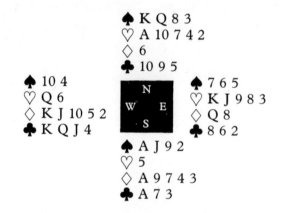

```
                    ♠ K Q 8 3
                    ♡ A 10 7 4 2
                    ◇ 6
                    ♣ 10 9 5
   ♠ 10 4                              ♠ 7 6 5
   ♡ Q 6              N                ♡ K J 9 8 3
   ◇ K J 10 5 2    W     E             ◇ Q 8
   ♣ K Q J 4          S                ♣ 8 6 2
                    ♠ A J 9 2
                    ♡ 5
                    ◇ A 9 7 4 3
                    ♣ A 7 3
```

You have no intention of allowing the opponents to score an over-ruff with the ten of spades. That would leave you with a maximum of seven trump tricks, which would still be enough. But when a trump is returned, two of your trumps disappear on the one trick and you make no more than six trump tricks—one down. You avoid this sorry outcome by ruffing the third heart with the jack of spades, which cannot be over-ruffed. You continue with a diamond and again you take no chance on being over-ruffed. You ruff with the queen of spades, ruff another heart with the ace of spades, and ruff a further diamond with the king of spades. You have made nine tricks and the position is:

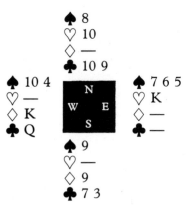

```
                    ♠ 8
                    ♡ 10
                    ◇ —
                    ♣ 10 9
        ♠ 10 4                   ♠ 7 6 5
        ♡ —         N             ♡ K
        ◇ K       W   E           ◇ —
        ♣ Q         S             ♣ —
                    ♠ 9
                    ♡ —
                    ◇ 9
                    ♣ 7 3
```

You make sure of your tenth trick by ruffing the ten of hearts with your nine of spades. Now it doesn't matter if West over-ruffs and returns a trump. The only trump you have left is dummy's eight of spades and it is big enough to score the tenth trick. East and West are welcome to queue up for the tricks that are left.

Here it is also a matter of a cross-ruff of sorts.

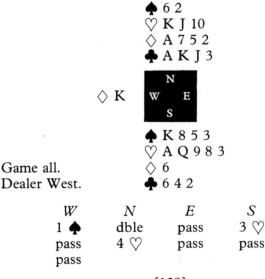

```
                    ♠ 6 2
                    ♡ K J 10
                    ◇ A 7 5 2
                    ♣ A K J 3
                        N
        ◇ K        W        E
                        S
                    ♠ K 8 5 3
                    ♡ A Q 9 8 3
Game all.           ◇ 6
Dealer West.        ♣ 6 4 2
```

W	N	E	S
1 ♠	dble	pass	3 ♡
pass	4 ♡	pass	pass
pass			

West leads the king of diamonds. Plan the play.

When you count your top tricks you arrive at a total of eight. The spade ace with East would allow you to make a trick with the king, and since you have escaped a trump lead you should be able to ruff at least one spade in dummy. The club finesse might provide an extra trick, and for that matter the suit could break 3–3, making the long club in dummy a winner.

At the table South won the first trick with the ace of diamonds and played a spade to his king. West won with the ace and made the obvious return of a trump. When dummy's remaining spade was played, West won again and returned another trump. It seemed best to take the spade ruff while the chance was there. When he had attended to that, South returned to hand with a diamond ruff and drew the last trump. The club finesse lost and the suit failed to break 3–3, for the complete deal was as follows:

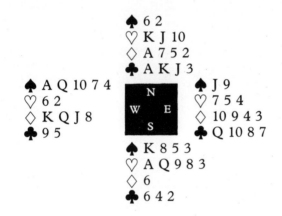

The breaks were not exactly friendly but the game should still have been made. Either South was an inexperienced player or he was afflicted by the complaint known as bridge-blindness. He missed the sure way of making his game.

South has three top tricks in the side suits and eight fat trumps. If he can produce seven tricks from the trumps he will be home.

Dummy's club honours are needed as entries, otherwise it

would be right to cash them immediately after winning the ace of diamonds. As it is, South ruffs a diamond at trick two, crosses to dummy with the ace of clubs, and ruffs another diamond. Next comes a club to the king, and when this stands up South is home and dry. He ruffs dummy's last diamond in hand and gets off lead with his third club.

The position is as follows:

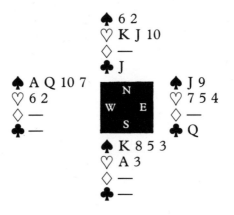

         ♠ 6 2
         ♡ K J 10
         ◇ —
         ♣ J

♠ A Q 10 7   ♠ J 9
♡ 6 2   ♡ 7 5 4
◇ —   ◇ —
♣ —   ♣ Q

         ♠ K 8 5 3
         ♡ A 3
         ◇ —
         ♣ —

Note that South has ruffed the three diamonds high to avoid all risk of an over-ruff.

So far East and West have been helpless witnesses to South's manoeuvres. East has just won the first defensive trick with the ten of clubs, and there are no more than two further tricks in spades for the defenders to take. No matter how the play goes, South can make sure of his tenth trick by ruffing the jack of clubs with his ace of hearts.

The only risk attached to South's line of play is that the clubs may be divided 5–1 or 6–0. One is often forced to take risks that are considerably greater.

♠ A K J 7 5
♡ 8 5 3
◇ A Q J 8 4
♣ —

♣ K

```
      N
  W       E
      S
```

♠ 3
♡ K Q 6
◇ K 10 9 2
♣ 10 8 4 3 2

Game all.
Dealer West.

South became declarer in five diamonds after West had opened with a bid of one club. The opening lead was the king of clubs. Your plan of play?

At the table South ruffed the club king in dummy and cashed the top spades, discarding the heart six from hand. He continued with a spade and ruffed with the nine of diamonds, hoping to fell the queen. But when West discarded the ten of hearts it was plain that no extra tricks could be established in spades. The king of hearts went to the ace, and West returned a trump on which East discarded a heart. South attempted to cash the queen of hearts, but West ruffed and returned another trump. Two down.

♠ A K J 7 5
♡ 8 5 3
◇ A Q J 8 4
♣ —

♠ 10 8   ♠ Q 9 6 4 2
♡ A 10   ♡ J 9 7 4 2
◇ 7 6 5 3   ◇ —
♣ A K J 6 5   ♣ Q 9 7

```
      N
  W       E
      S
```

♠ 3
♡ K Q 6
◇ K 10 9 2
♣ 10 8 4 3 2

Would you have made better use of your good fortune when you escaped an initial trump lead? The right play at trick two is to lead a heart to the king. Since you are short in spades and dummy short in clubs, a cross-ruff must be the safest line of play, and you know that in these situations you have to establish and cash your tricks in the side suits as quickly as possible. One heart trick and the top spades will give you three tricks in the side suits, leaving eight tricks to be made in trumps.

West will capture the king of hearts with the ace, but his trump switch comes too late. You win in dummy, play a heart to your queen, and then cash the ace and king of spades, discarding your heart loser. If all has gone well so far, you are home. You cross-ruff spades and clubs alternately, and when you have finished the defenders may have the last trick.

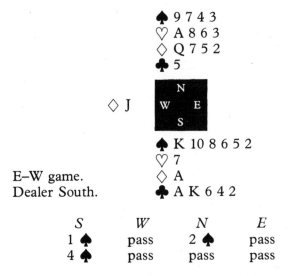

```
                    ♠ 9 7 4 3
                    ♡ A 8 6 3
                    ◇ Q 7 5 2
                    ♣ 5
                         N
            ◇ J      W        E
                         S
                    ♠ K 10 8 6 5 2
                    ♡ 7
E–W game.           ◇ A
Dealer South.       ♣ A K 6 4 2
```

S	W	N	E
1 ♠	pass	2 ♠	pass
4 ♠	pass	pass	pass

The jack of diamonds was led and South's singleton ace won. If the black suits broke favourably twelve tricks might be made. Full of optimism, South cashed the ace of clubs and ruffed a low club in dummy. When the queen appeared from East, South did not want to risk an over-ruff on the next

round. He therefore led a trump from the table. East showed
out, South played low, and West won with the jack.

West took a moment for thought. South clearly had a black
two-suiter and there could be nothing for the defenders in the
red suits. To protect his club strength West decided to
sacrifice a trump trick. He cashed the ace of spades and
continued with the queen. This removed the last trump from
dummy, and South eventually had to lose two club tricks to
go one down.

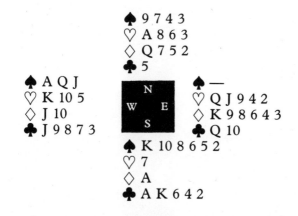

West produced a splendid defence but South was careless.
His thoughts should not have been on the possibility of
twelve tricks but on safeguarding his contract.

Do you see how he could have done this?

South should have left the trumps alone. There are only
three trumps out, and the defenders are welcome to score all
three as long as they make no tricks in the side suits.

After ruffing the club at trick three South should ruff a
diamond. The king of clubs is followed by another club ruff,
the ace of hearts is cashed, and a heart ruff puts South back in
hand. The fifth club is ruffed in dummy and another heart is
ruffed in hand. West has had to follow suit all the time and
South has already scored his ten tricks.

This is the position:

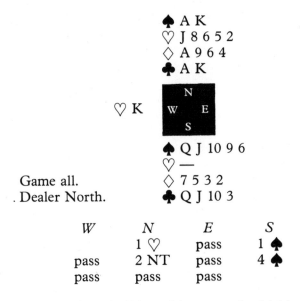

```
              ♠ 9
              ♡ —
              ◇ Q 7
              ♣ —
♠ A Q J    ┌─────────┐    ♠ —
♡ —        │    N    │    ♡ Q
◇ —        │ W     E │    ◇ K 9
♣ —        │    S    │    ♣ —
           └─────────┘
              ♠ K 10 8
              ♡ —
              ◇ —
              ♣ —
```

South plays a low spade from hand and West is obliged to concede the last trick to the king of spades. The cross-ruff not only ensures the contract but in this case produces an overtrick.

```
              ♠ A K
              ♡ J 8 6 5 2
              ◇ A 9 6 4
              ♣ A K
           ┌─────────┐
           │    N    │
♡ K        │ W     E │
           │    S    │
           └─────────┘
              ♠ Q J 10 9 6
              ♡ —
Game all.      ◇ 7 5 3 2
Dealer North.  ♣ Q J 10 3
```

W	N	E	S
	1 ♡	pass	1 ♠
pass	2 NT	pass	4 ♠
pass	pass	pass	

South ruffed the king of hearts and told himself that he would make ten tricks if the trumps broke 3–3. Seeing no better chance, he played off the ace and king of spades and then the ace and king of clubs. To return to his own hand he had to ruff a heart. If both defenders had been able to follow to the queen of spades South would have been all right, but in practice West showed out on the third round of trumps and East was able to ruff the third club. The complete deal:

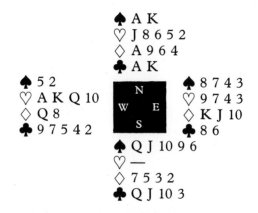

```
                  ♠ A K
                  ♡ J 8 6 5 2
                  ◇ A 9 6 4
                  ♣ A K
  ♠ 5 2                            ♠ 8 7 4 3
  ♡ A K Q 10         N             ♡ 9 7 4 3
  ◇ Q 8          W       E         ◇ K J 10
  ♣ 9 7 5 4 2        S             ♣ 8 6
                  ♠ Q J 10 9 6
                  ♡ —
                  ◇ 7 5 3 2
                  ♣ Q J 10 3
```

Relying on a 3–3 trump break was a pretty feeble effort on South's part. After ruffing the first trick he should have tested the clubs with the ace and king. Both will stand up as long as the division is no worse than 5–2. Having scored two clubs, South should cash the ace of diamonds. This will win as long as the suit is not divided 5–0. Having scored three tricks in the side suits, South can heave a sigh of relief and add up the score, for there is now no way for the contract to be defeated. The next six tricks are made on a high cross-ruff, and the defenders are welcome to their three tricks at the end.

Winner-On-Winner

"Loser-on-loser" is a well-known technique. "Winner-on-winner" is not so well known, but it is nevertheless effective. The idea is to manoeuvre the opponents into taking a trick twice over. A common outcome is that one defender is compelled to ruff his partner's winner.

```
                        ♠ 7 6 4
                        ♡ 8 5
                        ◇ A 8 4 2
                        ♣ A 8 4 3
                              N
            ♡ J        W          E
                              S
                        ♠ A K J 5 3 2
                        ♡ K Q 2
Game all.               ◇ 9
Dealer South.           ♣ J 6 2
```

S	W	N	E
1 ♠	pass	2 ♠	pass
3 ◇	pass	4 ♠	pass
pass	pass		

West leads the jack of hearts to his partner's ace and East returns the queen of diamonds. How do your thoughts run?

You have already lost a heart trick and it would take a great deal of luck to avoid two losers in clubs. The queen of spades is missing and the best chance, when holding nine cards, is to play for the drop.

The declarer who had the problem originally won the diamond return with dummy's ace and saw that it could not cost to ruff a diamond at trick three. Such precautions are taken automatically by experienced players. After ruffing the diamond South cashed the ace of spades on which West discarded a heart.

With East holding a sure trick in trumps there appeared to be four "inescapable" losers. South realised, however, that he might be able to produce ten tricks of his own before the defenders had time to make their four. The diamond ruff taken earlier had already set him on the way. This was the complete deal:

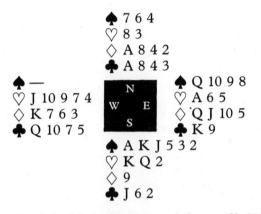

South cashed the king of hearts and then ruffed the queen of hearts to gain an extra entry to dummy. A diamond ruff was followed by a club to the ace and a further diamond ruff. The position had become:

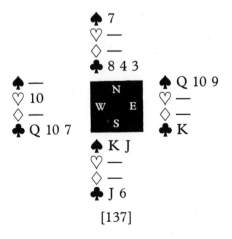

So far the defenders had scored only the ace of hearts and South had taken eight of his ten tricks. South simply got off lead with a club and waited for two further trump tricks. The last trick was won by the defenders in great style, East ruffing his partner's winning queen of clubs with the thirteenth trump.

The key to the whole manoeuvre lay in South's routine ruff of a diamond at trick three. Without the early ruff it would not have been possible to make the contract.

It is interesting to note that South's chosen line of play would have brought home the contract even if the East and West cards had been reversed, that is if West had held the double stopper in trumps.

In winner-on-winner declarer tries to arrange matters so that he can throw a loser when one defender ruffs while the other defender is forced to play a winner. An unhappy business for the defence.

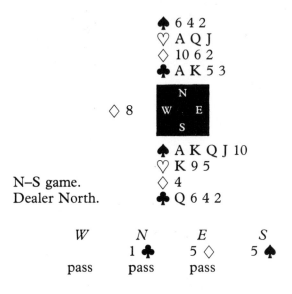

		♠ 6 4 2	
		♡ A Q J	
		◇ 10 6 2	
		♣ A K 5 3	

◇ 8

		♠ A K Q J 10	
N–S game.		♡ K 9 5	
Dealer North.		◇ 4	
		♣ Q 6 4 2	

W	N	E	S
	1 ♣	5 ◇	5 ♠
pass	pass	pass	

West led his partner's suit and South ruffed the second

diamond. On the ace of spades East discarded a diamond, revealing that the trumps lay as badly as they conceivably could. Well, South was not in a slam so he had a little breathing space. It hardly helped that West now had a trump more than South, but he might be held to just that one trump trick. If the clubs were 3–2 there would be no problem. It was necessary to guard against the possibility of a bad break in the suit. There would be no chance if West had a club trick. The distribution to protect against was a singleton club with West.

South cashed the queen of clubs and continued with a club towards the table. West, with no more clubs, could not find a winning defence. If he ruffed it would be at the expense of his partner's club trick and South would be able to play a loser from dummy. West therefore discarded a heart and the ace of clubs won. The complete deal was as follows:

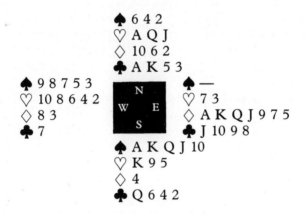

```
                 ♠ 6 4 2
                 ♡ A Q J
                 ◇ 10 6 2
                 ♣ A K 5 3
 ♠ 9 8 7 5 3        N        ♠ —
 ♡ 10 8 6 4 2   W       E    ♡ 7 3
 ◇ 8 3              S        ◇ A K Q J 9 7 5
 ♣ 7                         ♣ J 10 9 8
                 ♠ A K Q J 10
                 ♡ K 9 5
                 ◇ 4
                 ♣ Q 6 4 2
```

South continued with three rounds of hearts finishing in hand. Then another club was played towards dummy and West could only grind his teeth in frustration. Again he discarded, allowing the club king to win. Having scored three club tricks without loss, South cashed his high trumps and allowed the defenders to fight over the last trick.

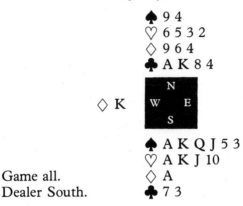

```
              ♠ 9 4
              ♡ 6 5 3 2
              ◇ 9 6 4
              ♣ A K 8 4
                   N
      ◇ K      W       E
                   S
              ♠ A K Q J 5 3
              ♡ A K J 10
              ◇ A
              ♣ 7 3
```

Game all.
Dealer South.

After an undisturbed bidding sequence South became declarer in a contract of six hearts. West led the king of diamonds. How would you plan the play?

At the table South tested the trumps immediately. It was gratifying when the queen of hearts dropped from West on the first round, but it was too early to rejoice. The distribution was clearly wild. Oh, well, if someone had the spades guarded they could have a trick. South was only in a small slam, after all.

South drew the rest of the trumps and cashed the ace of spades. When East showed out South realised, too late, that he was in trouble. He had no way of making more than four tricks in spades, which meant that the slam had to go one down. The complete deal:

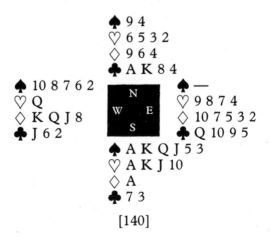

```
                  ♠ 9 4
                  ♡ 6 5 3 2
                  ◇ 9 6 4
                  ♣ A K 8 4
  ♠ 10 8 7 6 2         N          ♠ —
  ♡ Q                              ♡ 9 8 7 4
  ◇ K Q J 8       W       E        ◇ 10 7 5 3 2
  ♣ J 6 2             S            ♣ Q 10 9 5
                  ♠ A K Q J 5 3
                  ♡ A K J 10
                  ◇ A
                  ♣ 7 3
```

The cards certainly lay unfortunately for South but his play was careless. Once it had occurred to him that the spades as well as the hearts might be breaking badly, he should have found the way to protect himself.

When the queen of hearts appears on the first round, South can continue with the king to confirm the suspected 4–1 break. To avoid losing control, he now crosses to dummy with a club and plays a spade towards his hand. If both defenders follow he can draw the rest of the trumps and claim thirteen tricks. It is also a simple matter to make all the tricks if West shows out on the first spade. South cashes another top spade, ruffs a small spade in dummy and draws trumps.

On the actual lie of the cards it is East who is void in spades. If he ruffs, he is ruffing declarer's loser and his partner's winner. East discards a diamond, therefore, and South wins the ace of spades. Dummy is entered again in clubs and another spade is led. There is nothing East can do. If he refuses to ruff, South wins and ruffs a low spade on the table. East can make a trump trick but South makes his slam.

In Proper Order

One is often faced with the question of whether or not one can afford to safety-play a suit by applying the techniques described in the chapter on suit management. The answer may depend on what happens in the other suits.

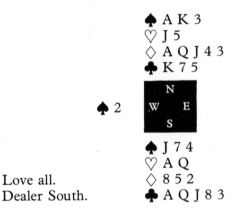

```
                     ♠ A K 3
                     ♡ J 5
                     ◊ A Q J 4 3
                     ♣ K 7 5
                          N
              ♠ 2    W         E
                          S
                     ♠ J 7 4
                     ♡ A Q
Love all.            ◊ 8 5 2
Dealer South.        ♣ A Q J 8 3
```

You become declarer in six no trumps and West leads the two of spades. Plan the play.

If the clubs are good for five tricks, as you expect, you will need only four tricks from the diamonds to make your slam. You have no use for a third trick in spades, and you would be taking a quite unnecessary risk if you played low from dummy at trick one.

What is the worst that could happen in clubs? The suit could divide 5–0 with West having the length. That would

[142]

leave you with only four club tricks and you would therefore
need to try for five tricks in diamonds. If East has five clubs?
No problem. You can finesse twice against the nine and the
ten to pick up the suit.

The first thing to do after winning the ace of spades, is to
test the clubs by cashing the king. You learn immediately how
the suit is divided:

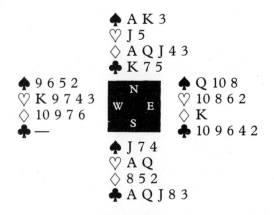

It doesn't bother you when West shows out on the first
club, for you know that you can score five tricks in the suit.
You also know that there is no need to try for five tricks in
diamonds—four will suffice. So you reject the idea of taking a
first-round finesse in diamonds. Instead you guard against
the possibility of a singleton king with East by playing off the
ace. The king drops and your problems are over. West is
given a diamond trick but you score the rest to make your
slam.

It is easy to make a false step on a hand like this. A declarer
who takes his eye off the ball for a moment might play a low
club to his ace at trick two. Ouch! Now there is no way of
making five club tricks. South is forced to go for the
maximum in diamonds by taking a first-round finesse. East
wins with the singleton king and returns a heart, and South
has to try the finesse since he has no more than eight tricks in
the minor suits. The finesse loses and a heart comes back, and
when the diamonds fail to break South has to be satisfied with
nine tricks—perhaps ten if he finds the end-play against East.
Two or three down, and all quite unnecessary.

The next problem is an old chestnut but one that deserves to be remembered. If the play is not so very instructive it is at any rate amusing.

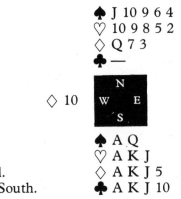

♠ J 10 9 6 4
♡ 10 9 8 5 2
◇ Q 7 3
♣ —

◇ 10

♠ A Q
♡ A K J
◇ A K J 5
♣ A K J 10

Love all.
Dealer South.

You are the declarer in a contract of six no trumps and West leads the ten of diamonds. How do you play to make sure of twelve tricks against any defence and distribution?

It is just a matter of taking things in proper order. You have nine top tricks and need to develop three more without losing control of any of your suits. The diamond queen is the only entry to dummy and must be preserved.

You win the opening lead in hand and play the queen of spades. The defenders cannot afford to take the king, for that would give you the three extra tricks you need in spades.

When the queen of spades is allowed to win, you need to develop only two extra tricks and you try a new gambit by leading the jack of hearts. If a defender wins with the queen, dummy's heart will provide the two tricks you need.

When the jack of hearts is allowed to win, you need to develop only one further trick, and you do that easily enough by playing the ten of clubs from hand. The queen of clubs is the only trick for the defence.

The complete deal:

In Proper Order

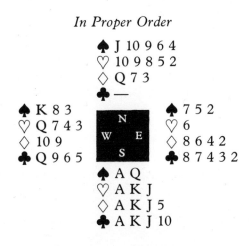

You lose control and lose the slam if you try to establish the spades by playing the ace first, or start the hearts by cashing the ace and king. Also, the suits must be tackled in the right order—spades first, then hearts and finally clubs—otherwise the slam cannot be made.

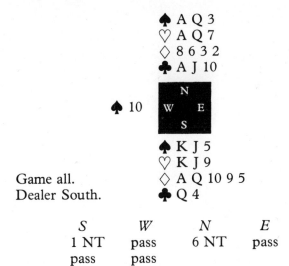

Game all.
Dealer South.

S	W	N	E
1 NT	pass	6 NT	pass
pass	pass		

West leads the ten of spades. How do you think this slam should be handled?

The duplication of values in the major suits is unfortunate. It means that you need six tricks from the minors to make the slam. The diamonds may break 2–2 with the king in the East hand, in which case a finesse of the queen will roll up the suit. Or East may have both honours guarded, in which case a double finesse in diamonds will be needed. West could have the singleton king, in which case if you start with the ace you will be able to take a subsequent finesse against the jack. In all these cases you are not concerned with the position of the king of clubs, for with five diamond tricks you need only one trick in clubs.

To make five tricks in diamonds you need not only to find a useful distribution of the cards but also to hit upon the winning line of play. The chances are not great.

But perhaps there is no need to depend on a friendly diamond position and a lucky guess?

You should start by finding out whether you have a club loser or not. Win the spade lead in your own hand and run the queen of clubs. If it wins, you know that you need only four tricks from the diamonds.

The complete deal:

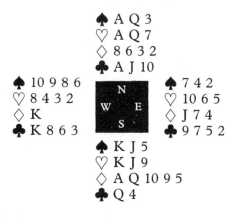

♠ A Q 3
♡ A Q 7
◇ 8 6 3 2
♣ A J 10

♠ 10 9 8 6   ♠ 7 4 2
♡ 8 4 3 2   ♡ 10 6 5
◇ K   ◇ J 7 4
♣ K 8 6 3   ♣ 9 7 5 2

♠ K J 5
♡ K J 9
◇ A Q 10 9 5
♣ Q 4

When it transpires that you have no club loser you can afford to safety-play the diamonds. You therefore start with the ace. If both defenders follow suit with small cards, you cross to dummy in either major and continue with a low diamond towards your hand. You have eliminated the risk of a misguess, since the card played by East on the second round will solve your problem.

Without the safety play in diamonds you would need to do some good guessing. If you start with a finesse of the queen and lose to the king, you will not know whether to play for the drop or finesse again on the second round. You will have a similar awkward guess on the second round if you start with a finesse of the ten and lose to the jack.

As the cards lie, the safety play is rewarded by an overtrick. The king falls under your ace and you subsequently score five diamond tricks by finessing against the jack.

If the queen of clubs had lost to the king, you would not have been able to afford a safety play in diamonds but would have had to play for the maximum. The best chance is to begin with a finesse of the queen. If West follows with a small card you continue with the ace. If the jack appears from West on the first round, you return to dummy for a further finesse against the king.

Be sure that you appreciate the need to test the clubs first in order to find out how to tackle the diamonds.

The Small Details

This hand is rather similar to an example we looked at earlier in the book:

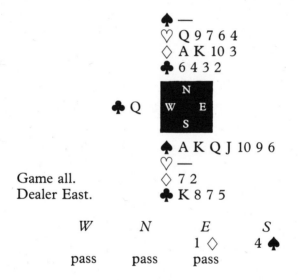

♠ —
♡ Q 9 7 6 4
◇ A K 10 3
♣ 6 4 3 2

♣ Q

♠ A K Q J 10 9 6
♡ —
◇ 7 2
♣ K 8 7 5

Game all.
Dealer East.

W	N	E	S
		1 ◇	4 ♠
pass	pass	pass	

In the earlier hand one of South's small clubs was on the table. This little detail makes a big difference.

West led the queen of clubs to his partner's ace and East returned the nine of clubs. How would you plan the play?

At the table South saw no danger and covered with the king of clubs. West ruffed and returned a heart. South ruffed and rattled off his trumps, but East had no difficulty in keeping the right cards and the contract had to go one down.

It looks as though it should make no difference whether South plays the king of clubs at trick two or later. It is bound to be ruffed out anyway. True, but the careful general tries to protect himself against all sorts of surprises. A 4–1 club break is not so very unlikely.

If the clubs are 3–2, South gives up an overtrick by refusing to play the king of clubs at trick two. In return he receives a chance of making the contract when West's club queen is a singleton. The complete deal:

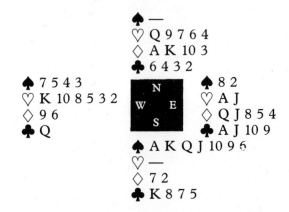

```
                   ♠ —
                   ♡ Q 9 7 6 4
                   ◇ A K 10 3
                   ♣ 6 4 3 2
 ♠ 7 5 4 3           N          ♠ 8 2
 ♡ K 10 8 5 3 2   W     E       ♡ A J
 ◇ 9 6               S          ◇ Q J 8 5 4
 ♣ Q                            ♣ A J 10 9
                   ♠ A K Q J 10 9 6
                   ♡ —
                   ◇ 7 2
                   ♣ K 8 7 5
```

South lets the nine of clubs win and West discards something. Naturally East continues with another club, and now it is time to play the king. West ruffs, and it makes no difference what he returns. By keeping his king of clubs for the third round, the careful general has rectified the count for a squeeze. The tempo is right and South plays off trumps to reach this position:

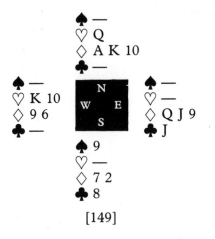

```
            ♠ —
            ♡ Q
            ◇ A K 10
            ♣ —
 ♠ —          N          ♠ —
 ♡ K 10    W     E       ♡ —
 ◇ 9 6        S          ◇ Q J 9
 ♣ —                     ♣ J
            ♠ 9
            ♡ —
            ◇ 7 2
            ♣ 8
```

When South plays his last trump and discards the queen of hearts from the table, East has to surrender. Two clubs and a ruff are the only tricks for the defence.

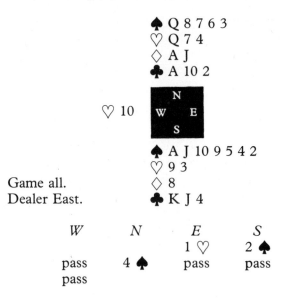

♠ Q 8 7 6 3
♡ Q 7 4
◇ A J
♣ A 10 2

♡ 10

♠ A J 10 9 5 4 2
♡ 9 3
◇ 8
♣ K J 4

Game all.
Dealer East.

W	N	E	S
		1 ♡	2 ♠
pass	4 ♠	pass	pass
pass			

West led the ten of hearts and dummy played low. East overtook with the jack to continue with the king and then the ace of hearts. South considered discarding a club on the third heart. He would then succeed if East had the king of spades, or if East failed to play a fourth heart to promote a trick for his partner's king of trumps. South rejected this idea, however; West might have a third heart, after all, or he might be unable to over-ruff. South therefore played a low trump on the third round of hearts. West over-ruffed and returned a diamond.
The complete deal:

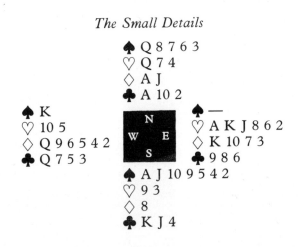

```
              ♠ Q 8 7 6 3
              ♡ Q 7 4
              ◇ A J
              ♣ A 10 2
♠ K                        ♠ —
♡ 10 5          N          ♡ A K J 8 6 2
◇ Q 9 6 5 4 2  W   E       ◇ K 10 7 3
♣ Q 7 5 3         S        ♣ 9 8 6
              ♠ A J 10 9 5 4 2
              ♡ 9 3
              ◇ 8
              ♣ K J 4
```

South won the diamond switch with the ace. He needed the rest of the tricks and his only problem was to locate the queen of clubs. South rattled off a number of trumps but the discards gave no clue. When the moment of decision came, he took the view that the key card was likely to be in the hand that opened the bidding. He therefore took a second-round finesse against East and the result was one down.

South missed a small detail. He could have made sure of his contract by ruffing the third heart with the ace of spades. He continues with a diamond to the ace and a diamond ruff before exiting in spades, and it makes no difference who has the king.

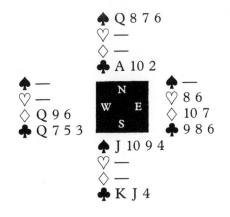

```
              ♠ Q 8 7 6
              ♡ —
              ◇ —
              ♣ A 10 2
♠ —                       ♠ —
♡ —            N          ♡ 8 6
◇ Q 9 6       W   E       ◇ 10 7
♣ Q 7 5 3        S        ♣ 9 8 6
              ♠ J 10 9 4
              ♡ —
              ◇ —
              ♣ K J 4
```

West is on lead and must either return a club or concede a ruff and discard. If East had been able to win the trump trick he would have been in exactly the same position.

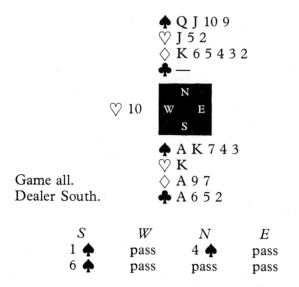

♠ Q J 10 9
♡ J 5 2
◇ K 6 5 4 3 2
♣ —

♡ 10

♠ A K 7 4 3
♡ K
◇ A 9 7
♣ A 6 5 2

Game all.
Dealer South.

S	W	N	E
1 ♠	pass	4 ♠	pass
6 ♠	pass	pass	pass

After a brief bidding sequence South became declarer in six spades. West led the ten of hearts and East played the ace, felling South's king. The queen of clubs was returned, South winning with the ace and discarding a heart from dummy. On the play of a low trump West discarded a club, revealing the dreaded 4–0 trump break. South quickly realised that he no longer had any chance of making the contract, even if the diamonds were 2–2. He needed the rest of the tricks, but his own small diamonds were high enough to block the suit—something he should have noticed at the beginning. The complete deal:

```
                    ♠ Q J 10 9
                    ♡ J 5 2
                    ◇ K 6 5 4 3 2
                    ♣ —
   ♠ —                            ♠ 8 6 5 2
   ♡ 10 9 8 6 3      N            ♡ A Q 7 4
   ◇ Q 10         W     E         ◇ J 8
   ♣ K 9 8 7 4 3     S            ♣ Q J 10
                    ♠ A K 7 4 3
                    ♡ K
                    ◇ A 9 7
                    ♣ A 6 5 2
```

Do you see how South could have avoided the blockage?

It was right to win the ace of clubs when East returned the queen at trick two. South's mistake lay in discarding a heart from the table.

An inescapable requirement for the success of the slam is that the diamonds are 2–2. The only possibility of over-coming the annoying blockage is for South to discard one of his diamonds on dummy's trumps. In order to do that he needs to reduce his own trumps by ruffing twice, and the only suit he can ruff is hearts. When South discarded a heart from dummy at trick two, he destroyed his own ruffing possibilities. He can afford to discard a diamond from dummy, since five diamond tricks, four trumps in dummy, two ruffs in hand plus the ace of clubs will bring his total up to the required twelve tricks.

Accordingly the plan should be to win the ace of clubs, discarding a diamond from the table, and play a spade to dummy's queen. The 4–0 trump break proves that this foresight was necessary. South ruffs a heart with the ace of spades, cashes the ace of diamonds and crosses to dummy with the diamond king. When both defenders follow suit, the slam is home and dry. South ruffs the remaining heart with the king of spades and plays off the rest of the trumps. On dummy's last trump he discards the blocking diamond from his hand, and the rest of the tricks are won by the three established diamonds on the table.

The little detail of retaining the apparently-worthless hearts in dummy makes the difference between the success and the failure of the slam.

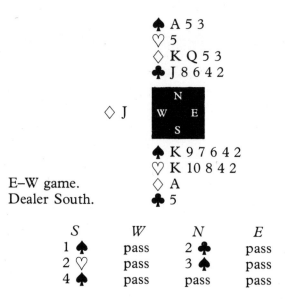

```
              ♠ A 5 3
              ♡ 5
              ◇ K Q 5 3
              ♣ J 8 6 4 2
                     N
      ◇ J    W         E
                     S
              ♠ K 9 7 6 4 2
              ♡ K 10 8 4 2
              ◇ A
              ♣ 5
```

E–W game.
Dealer South.

S	W	N	E
1 ♠	pass	2 ♣	pass
2 ♡	pass	3 ♠	pass
4 ♠	pass	pass	pass

West leads the jack of diamonds and East follows with the two. Your plan of play?

For some reason there is a great temptation to cross to the ace of spades and hasten to discard the club loser from hand. That line of play does not work so well when the complete deal turns out to be:

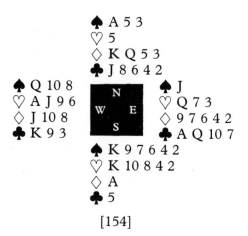

```
                  ♠ A 5 3
                  ♡ 5
                  ◇ K Q 5 3
                  ♣ J 8 6 4 2
    ♠ Q 10 8                    ♠ J
    ♡ A J 9 6       N           ♡ Q 7 3
    ◇ J 10 8    W       E       ◇ 9 7 6 4 2
    ♣ K 9 3         S           ♣ A Q 10 7
                  ♠ K 9 7 6 4 2
                  ♡ K 10 8 4 2
                  ◇ A
                  ♣ 5
```

When the deal was played, South was quick to get rid of his club loser in this manner. Then he played a heart to the king and ace. West naturally returned a spade to knock out the king. South was able to ruff one heart in dummy and discard another on a diamond, but he still had to lose two more hearts and a trump for one down.

South's long hearts are so feeble that he ought to make sure of his ruffs in dummy. He should pave the way at trick two by playing a low heart from hand. He would prefer to play from dummy, of course, but beggars cannot be choosers. To use the ace of spades as an entry is an unsafety play of the first magnitude.

When South gives up the heart, the defenders can cash one club trick and then do best by switching to trumps. Dummy's ace wins and two of South's hearts are discarded on the diamond honours. The other two can be ruffed with dummy's small trumps. South has club ruffs as entries to his own hand, and West is unable to score more than the one trump trick that is his due.

```
              ♠ 7
              ♡ A K J
              ◇ 8 7 6
              ♣ A 8 7 6 5 2
                  ┌─────────┐
                  │    N    │
      ♠ 5         │ W     E │
                  │    S    │
                  └─────────┘
              ♠ K 9 2
              ♡ Q 6 4 3
  N–S game.    ◇ K 2
  Dealer North. ♣ K J 10 4
```

With no interference from the opponents, South becomes declarer in a contract of three no trumps. West leads the five of spades to his partner's ace and the jack of spades is returned. You win with the king, West plays the four, and you discard a diamond from dummy. When you cash the three heart tricks in dummy, East discards the four of diamonds on the third round. How should you continue?

You observe that West appears to have started with at least

five spades and that he has also shown up with four hearts. In that case he can hardly have a club stopper, for it is unthinkable that East would have remained silent with a seven-card or longer diamond suit. What you must guard against, therefore, is a distribution something like the following:

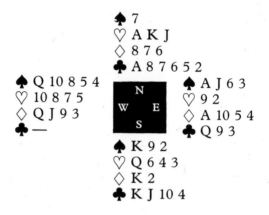

♠ 7
♡ A K J
◇ 8 7 6
♣ A 8 7 6 5 2

♠ Q 10 8 5 4
♡ 10 8 7 5
◇ Q J 9 3
♣ —

♠ A J 6 3
♡ 9 2
◇ A 10 5 4
♣ Q 9 3

♠ K 9 2
♡ Q 6 4 3
◇ K 2
♣ K J 10 4

You test the clubs by cashing dummy's ace, and there is no problem about how to continue. But there is a small detail that might easily be overlooked. On the ace of clubs you should unblock the jack or the ten from your hand. When West shows out on the first round, you finesse against East's queen and cash the king. Your four of clubs is then worth its weight in gold as an entry to the remaining clubs on the table. Although it is only a matter of overtricks this time, there is no reason to spurn overtricks when they can safely be made.

Look Out For Trojan Horses

Don't trust your opponents any further than you have to. They are straining every nerve to get the better of you, as is apparent from some of the examples we have seen. Although the connection with safety play may not be obvious, it is as well to bear in mind some of the well-known ways of confusing opponents and setting them on the wrong track.

Because a finesse wins, for instance, it does not necessarily mean that a repeated finesse will have equal success.

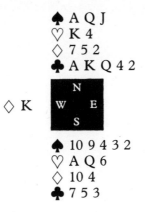

```
              ♠ A Q J
              ♡ K 4
              ◇ 7 5 2
              ♣ A K Q 4 2
                   N
      ◇ K     W         E
                   S
              ♠ 10 9 4 3 2
              ♡ A Q 6
Game all.     ◇ 10 4
Dealer North. ♣ 7 5 3
```

Against silent opponents you become declarer in a contract of four spades. The defenders attack in diamonds and you ruff the third round. You start on the trumps, playing a low spade to dummy's queen which wins the trick. How should you continue?

[157]

It appears that you can return to hand in hearts without risk and play another spade for a finesse of the jack. The apparent lack of risk is an illusion, however, and if you play like that you have let yourself be fooled. The complete deal:

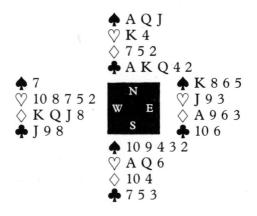

```
              ♠ A Q J
              ♡ K 4
              ◇ 7 5 2
              ♣ A K Q 4 2
♠ 7                        ♠ K 8 6 5
♡ 10 8 7 5 2    N          ♡ J 9 3
◇ K Q J 8    W   E         ◇ A 9 6 3
♣ J 9 8         S          ♣ 10 6
              ♠ 10 9 4 3 2
              ♡ A Q 6
              ◇ 10 4
              ♣ 7 5 3
```

When you play a second trump towards dummy you learn that West started with a singleton. You are now beyond the point of no return. If you put up the ace and continue with the jack, East will win and force you with a diamond, establishing a second trump trick for himself. Nor can you do better by finessing the jack on the second round. East will win and return a heart, and with the spades blocked you will be unable to draw East's fourth trump. You may try using the clubs as reserve-trumps, but East can ruff the third round while you are obliged to follow suit.

To protect yourself against any possible deception on East's part, you should continue with the jack of spades from dummy on the second round. This retains control and leaves the defence helpless. East may win, but you have the ace of spades in dummy to take care of a further diamond lead. If East returns a heart, you win in dummy and unblock the ace of spades. The heart entry to your hand is still intact, enabling you to draw the last trump and claim the rest of the tricks.

East cannot gain by holding up his king of spades a second time. In that case you continue with the ace of spades and make use of the clubs as reserve-trumps, playing clubs until East ruffs with his master trump. East may ruff whenever he pleases, but the defenders score no more than two diamonds and the king of spades.

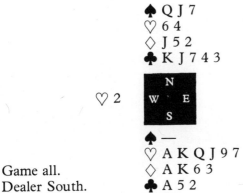

♠ Q J 7
♡ 6 4
♢ J 5 2
♣ K J 7 4 3

♡ 2

♠ —
♡ A K Q J 9 7
♢ A K 6 3
♣ A 5 2

Game all.
Dealer South.

After an undisturbed bidding sequence you arrive in a contract of six hearts. West leads the two of hearts and it's up to you. How do you plan to bring home the slam?

At the table South drew the outstanding trumps in three rounds, West discarding a spade. Then South turned his attention to the clubs, cashing the ace and continuing with a second club on which West played the queen. Dummy's king won, the jack of clubs drew the remaining card in the suit, and the slam was made with an overtrick. Any comments?

The above description of the course of events is what South expected to happen. In sober fact the complete deal was as follows:

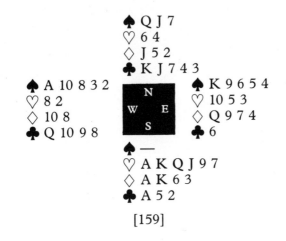

♠ Q J 7
♡ 6 4
♢ J 5 2
♣ K J 7 4 3

♠ A 10 8 3 2
♡ 8 2
♢ 10 8
♣ Q 10 9 8

♠ K 9 6 5 4
♡ 10 5 3
♢ Q 9 7 4
♣ 6

♠ —
♡ A K Q J 9 7
♢ A K 6 3
♣ A 5 2

[159]

South thought his eyes were at fault when East discarded a spade on the second round of clubs. Gradually it came home to him that he had fallen into West's trap. West still had a sure stopper in clubs and the suit was worth only three tricks to South. There was still a chance that West had the queen of diamonds or that the diamonds would break 3–3. South ruffed himself back to hand and played a low diamond to dummy's jack. East won and returned a spade for South to ruff. South cashed his remaining trump, but the defenders had no difficulty in keeping the right cards and East's nine of diamonds eventually took the setting trick.

South should not have allowed himself to be deceived. He should have played low from dummy on the second round of clubs, for by so doing he could guarantee his contract. Giving up the chance of an overtrick is a trifling price to pay.

It would have been easier for South to spot the safe way of handling the suit if West had played a small club on the second round. Again it is right to play low from dummy, refusing the finesse in order to guard against the possibility of West holding all the remaining clubs.